慈悲
時時歡喜，處處安身

靜思心靈小語

釋證嚴——著

李屏賓——攝影

目　錄

序
心蓮萬蕊，締造愛的社會　　　　　　　　　　　　釋證嚴　004

前　言
一念心，剎那即永恆　　　　　　　　　　　　　　李屏賓　010

緣起
慈悲
016

慈悲，是真正的愛，是「無緣大慈，同體大悲」，不只是愛人，更要愛天地萬物與眾生。所以，要用心了解人與周遭事、物、大地、氣候的關係，將好的能量從家庭向社會延伸，啟動人人大腦的「慈悲利他」區，以身形做典範，帶動善循環。

Part 1. 慈：給予眾生安樂 　　　　　　　　　*018*

慈就是愛，是清淨的大愛。「無緣大慈」，是指沒有污染的愛：他與我雖然非親非故，而我卻能愛他；愛得他快樂，我也沒煩惱，這就是清淨的大愛。

——《靜思語・第一集》

Part 2. 悲：拔除眾生痛苦 　　　　　　　　　*122*

悲即是同情心。能互相寬諒、容忍，表現一分寬心、愛心，即是悲心。最幸福的人生，就是能寬容與悲憫一切眾生的人生。

——《靜思語・第一集》

後　記
慈悲最本真的樣貌　　　　　　　　　　　　　蔡青兒　*226*

序

心蓮萬蕊，締造愛的社會

釋證嚴

二〇二五年一月二十一日，嘉義大埔發生六‧四級強震，鄰近的台南市楠西、玉井受創嚴重，上千戶房屋受損。一如往常，慈濟得訊立時啟動救援行動——提供物資協助市府安置災民、供應熱食，啟動安心關懷、發放應急金，農曆年後更積極展開受損房屋的修繕，並規畫永久屋等。

究竟是什麼力量，支持慈濟人義無反顧地投入吃力不討好的事呢？是慈濟人心中最堅定的信念。

慈濟，是「慈悲為懷，濟世救人」，從一九六六年成立至今，這八個字就是慈濟人人心中最堅定的信念。

「慈」是予樂，「悲」是拔苦

把別人的苦難視為自己的苦難，別人的孤單、老、殘、病、窮，都當成是自己切身之事；不忌語言、膚色、習慣、信仰，普天下所有人都視如自己的親人。我希望的境界，願與他共享；他的快樂就是我的快樂，他的苦難，我願承擔部分，與他同甘共苦，這種「同理心，即是慈悲等觀」。

序

這種大愛,不只愛自己,也不拘泥只有認識的親友鄰居同儕自己人而已;他的愛已經開闊到普天之下,這叫做大愛入人群。時時刻刻持同理心,更要生生世世持四等心,也就是諸法平等、發心平等、道心平等、慈悲平等,這四種平等心。將近六十年來,都是抱持這樣的信念。慈濟人不為名利,即便在脆弱、遭受各種風風雨雨時,仍舊不改初衷,無所求的關心與付出,帶給別人快樂,膚慰別人的哀傷。

長期旅居加拿大,樂意將列治文市一方很好的土地捐給慈濟、成立愛心農場的邵明路先生:十多年前,他讀到《慧語流泉》這本書,看了非常感動和敬佩。這份感動一直放在心上,歷久彌新。慈濟加拿大分會現任執行長苗萬輝與邵明路、臧若華夫婦聊天時,訝異《慧語流泉》這本書對他影響之大,對這本書的內容很好奇;於是上網查看有無出售,哪怕是二手書都願意高價請購。他說,閱讀後發現,這本書的內容,師父對大家所講的話,或者最近大家正在閱讀的《靜思法髓妙蓮華》套書,所講的內容方向都是一致的。當時我回說:「珍

貴就在這裡!」

時間是最好的考驗。書的作者與他所堅持的信念都是一致的,更重要的是,經過時間長河的淬煉,還有時代變遷與世間的考驗,方向還是一致的,這就是真正的經典,值得遵循與實踐的理念。

簡單一句話,影響一生

近幾年來,因為校園紛紛設置靜思閱讀書軒,聽到青兒分享許多《靜思語》對兒童與青少年產生的影響。

有國中女生說:「不要小看自己,因為人有無限的可能。」這句話深深影響了她,成為她面對困難時的力量支柱。熱愛跆拳道的她說,最困難的就是遇到挫折時能否維持堅定的心,她曾經多次想要放棄,尤其受傷或低潮時,因為《靜思語》的鼓勵,她會提醒自己,已經付出這麼多的努力,就不要輕易放棄,撐過了這些磨難,最終的成果必然會更加甜美。

序

　　還有一位國小男生，非常叛逆，大家對他都很頭痛。後來學校開始採用靜思語教學，這位學生透過閱讀《靜思語》有了很大的改變，校方還把他的成長歷程拍成影片，令人驚豔。他說，《靜思語》有兩句話影響他很深，一句是：「對父母盡孝，是人生最大的福氣。」他想，不讓父母操心，就是盡大孝。另一句是：「小事不做，大事難成。」他表示會努力、慢慢的改，不再讓父母操心。

　　書籍的價值在於「有用」，就是能夠利益人群。去年是《靜思語》出版三十五周年，已經翻譯二十四種語文，不同宗教、不同種族、不同國度，透過不同的形式，發揮極大的影響力。《靜思語》深入淺出，就是靜思系統的《大藏經》，簡單的一句話，影響多少的人生！就是一念之間，也是一句話之間，同樣可以教育人間。看到《靜思語》慢慢深入並且影響我們的下一代，這就是書籍發揮它的良能，也是最有利益人群的用途。這都是佛法入人間，也是靜思在人間。

長養慈悲心，心靈風光美人文

不知不覺間，《靜思心靈小語》系列的書已經出版第三本了。一句句的靜思語，因為一張張的照片，不僅增加美觀；同時為靜思語作出詮釋，而鮮明活躍起來。每一句靜思語都能沉澱咀嚼，每張照片也都詮釋天地之美。抬頭望天是同一片天，低頭看地都在同一個地球，只是空間拉大，所以他的空間可以跟我的空間又會合，因為用了靜思語。

書中的照片，都是從攝影家李屏賓居士拍攝幾千張照片挑選出來的，文字很簡潔，但都值得咀嚼回味；配上靈動的照片，文字也有了意象。很感恩李居士慷慨提供數千張極為珍貴的照片，因為篇幅所限，只能忍痛割捨。希望這一系列的書，在咀嚼文字之餘，欣賞美麗的照片，感受那分心靈風光之美，也在心中長養慈悲心懷。

前言

一念心,剎那即永恆

李屏賓

這系列的第一本《愛，最好的祝福：靜思心靈小語》書裡，有一句我覺得很有深意的靜思語：「只要緣深，不怕緣來得遲；只要找到路，就不怕路遙遠。」無論是我與上人、與青兒或是與慈濟之間，深深的緣，似乎早就埋藏在我生命的旅途中。

　　認識青兒十幾年，這些年每次經過台北，我們都會小聚。多年前回台探望母親時，曾陪伴母親面見上人。我與上人見面的機會不多，以為上人應該不記得我。沒想到上人總記得我，還時常問青兒，我什麼時候會回來（靜思精舍），心中備感溫暖，覺得無論我到世界的哪個角落，總有一處安頓心靈的歸處。

打開觀看「攝影」的新視野

　　我覺得自己年輕的時候，心裡就開始有上人所講的愛、善（剛好就是前兩本書的主題），一直默默在走這個路上。有一次，上人講到皈依時的一段話，讓我印象非常深刻。

　　上人說：「皈依其實沒什麼特別，就是一念心。這

前　言

一念心,就是信。信,要相信人間的正理,正向的道理認清楚就不會偏。」上人以我為例:「就如你的照相機,要拍一個美的環境要很用心,而且鏡頭要如何對準:有功夫的對準,每一張都很漂亮;沒有功夫的,差之毫里,失之千里。所以正道、正方向是很重要的,就如你的鏡頭一樣。」

上人還說:「……世間很複雜,我們要選擇善的方向,還更需要方法,只要選擇對的專長,人間會合起來,那就是美。皈依,就是皈依佛,佛陀的覺悟,我們的信念。相信的念頭,就是信佛。還要信法;人人都有方法,你的方法,是美好的境界;我的方法,是引導的境界;大家的方法,是如何讓人間有生機,各有事業,人間有生機,都要回歸善與正、真誠的心,所以人人都要有真誠的心。真,人人行善,那就是美。你也有法,美化人間;我也有法,我用說的來美化人間,大家善法集中,就是佛陀對我們的教育。」上人這段話,打開我觀看「攝影」這個專業與藝術的另一個視野。

攝影，一念心

　　皈依，只是一念心；攝影，也是一念心。我在《光，帶我走向遠方》這本書裡曾經寫到，自己如何在許多工作與電影的幕後，成為「一個人」，「一個人的難關，一個人的孤獨，一個人的江湖，我已然是當代的獨孤不敗，這對我後來的人生影響很大。當我被留滯金門、綠島獨行、遣放漢城、流浪香港、河內夜行、單騎赴日、遠戰巴黎，還有一個人的大雪清晨……」

　　在這許許多多的「一個人」的時刻，為了紓壓而隨手拍攝的照片，蘊藏了許多我不為人知的心境，面臨的人生困境、壓力與煩惱。拍攝當時的一念心，剎那即是永恆。《愛，最好的祝福：靜思心靈小語》的封面照片，就是我在拍攝電影《長江圖》時，逆著幾千里長又風雨難測的長江而上，只能前進不能回頭、也不能轉彎的時刻所拍攝，象徵了時間的流逝，人生沒有回頭路，且處處都是挑戰，要如何克服未知的危機。

前言

從微小之物的強大生命力,感受慈悲

慈悲,是感受自己與萬物相互依存,找回自己最溫暖的那一念心。這些於世界各地捕捉的瞬間精采,無論是兒童、老人、落葉、樹林、雲朵、昆蟲、野花、湖泊、沙漠或建築,都是拍攝當下的心情紀錄,最質樸、也未經處理。這次選出的照片中,很多都是有天有地的、綻放自己光芒與美麗的小野花,即便弱小、卑微、不起眼,依舊散發蓬勃的生命力,代表的是生命堅強的力量,以及上天對萬事萬物的慈悲。

我所知道的《靜思語》,既真實又親和、既深邃又淺白;很少是「驚人之語」,卻經常「一言點醒夢中人」,大多是從現實人生裡出發,從個人實踐中體悟,啟發了很多人的智慧與善念。

緣分,真的非常奇妙。我認識青兒這麼久,也很早就知道《靜思語》,但我從沒想到當初與青兒分享的照片,有一天會結合上人的智慧法語集結成冊,出版成書。希望透過影像與文字的交織,讓書中的每一幅畫面

與每一句話語,引領大家進入一場心靈與視覺的沉澱之旅,從中獲得寧靜與啟發。

慈悲

慈悲，本為佛教用語。慈，指給予眾生安樂；悲，指拔除眾生的痛苦。後轉為慈愛、悲憫的意思。慈愛，仁慈且富有愛心；悲憫，慈悲憐憫。

「時時保持快樂的心境，把快樂的氣氛散布給四周的人，此即『慈』；眾生有苦難能及時為其拔除，此即『悲』。」（錄自《靜思語‧第二集》）

慈悲，是真正的愛，是「無緣大慈，同體大悲」，不只是愛人，更要愛天地萬物與眾生。所以，要用心了解人與周遭事、物、大地、氣候的關係，將好的能量從家庭向社會延伸，啟動人人大腦的「慈悲利他」區，以身形做典範，帶動善循環。

Part 1

慈：給予眾生安樂

慈就是愛，是清淨的大愛。「無緣大慈」，是指沒有污染的愛：他與我雖然非親非故，而我卻能愛他；愛得他快樂，我也沒煩惱，這就是清淨的大愛。

——《靜思語・第一集》

Unconditional loving-kindness is love that is free of defilements. Although you and I are complete strangers, I can still love you in such a way that you feel happy, while I am also without afflictions. This is pure, great love.

Part 1
慈：給予眾生安樂

「軟實力」，是軟性的力量，是用愛深入人心，接引人在愛的大環境中，潛移默化洗淨心地。

——《靜思語·孝為人本》

The "soft power" of love penetrates hearts and leads people into an environment of love that will subtly affect them and purify their hearts.

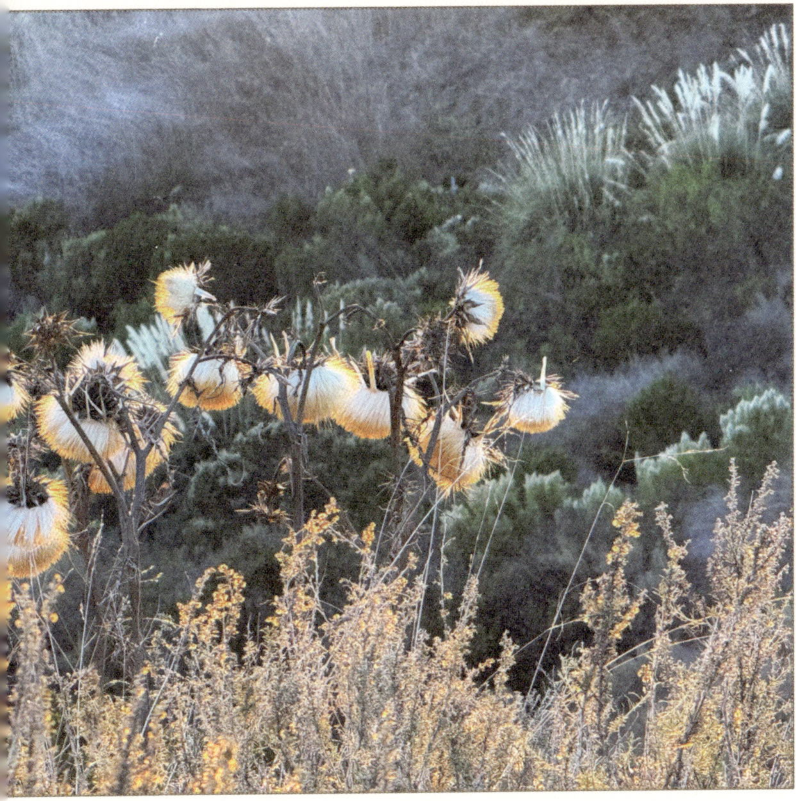

Part 1
慈：給予眾生安樂

無色彩的愛——「時」不計長短，「地」不分遠近，「人」不分宗教與種族，只要有苦難，我們看得到、聽得到、做得到，都應盡量去付出，絕無希求回報的心念。愛得普遍，愛得透徹，愛得乾淨俐落，就是「無緣大慈，同體大悲」的純淨真愛。

——《靜思語‧第二集》

Love transcends time and space, religion, and ethnicity. No matter when or where people are suffering, if we can reach out to help, we must do everything we can without expecting anything in return. Such unconditional and universal love is the most pure and simple.

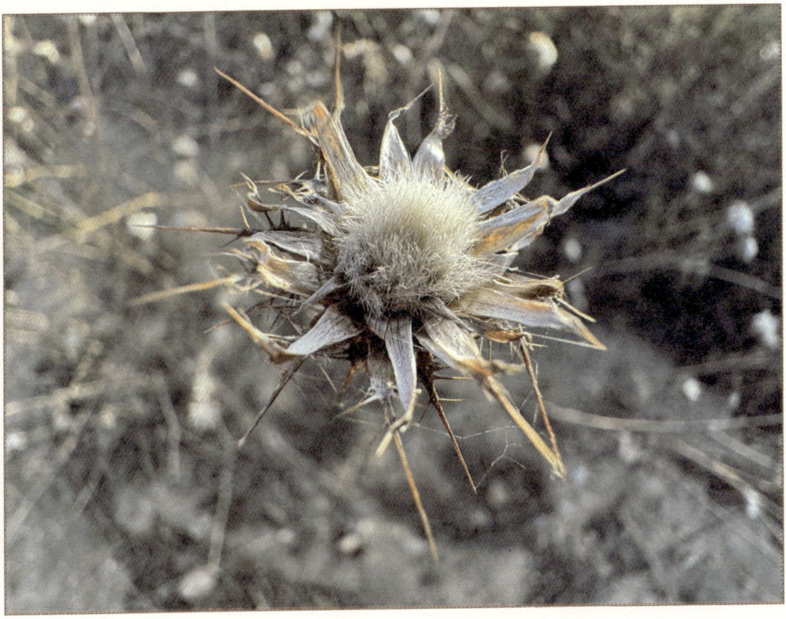

Part 1
慈：給予眾生安樂

長白山天池附近

沒有數字的代價,即為「無量」。不辭勞苦的付出,便是「大慈悲」。付出勞力又服務得很歡喜,便叫做「喜捨」。

——《靜思語・第一集》

The Four Infinite Minds are loving-kindness, compassion, joy, and equanimity. "Infinite" describes something which cannot be measured with numbers. Willingly enduring hardship for the sake of helping others is the practice of great loving-kindness and compassion. Making an effort to joyfully help others is the practice of giving with joy and equanimity.

Part 1

慈：給予眾生安樂

慈悲喜捨這四個字，分開而言：慈喜是予樂，是教富；而悲捨是拔苦，是濟貧。

——《靜思語·第一集》

Of the Four Infinite Minds, "loving-kindness," paired with "joy" teaches us to give joy. This is the practice of teaching the rich. "Compassion" paired with "equanimity" teaches us to relieve suffering. This is the practice of helping the poor.

Part 1
慈：給予眾生安樂

佛陀講慈悲，是以愛心仁德爲體，以誠正和睦爲用。

——《靜思語・第一集》

The Buddha teaches that to practice compassion is to apply the principles of sincerity, integrity, and harmony in our practice while embodying love, benevolence, and virtue in our actions.

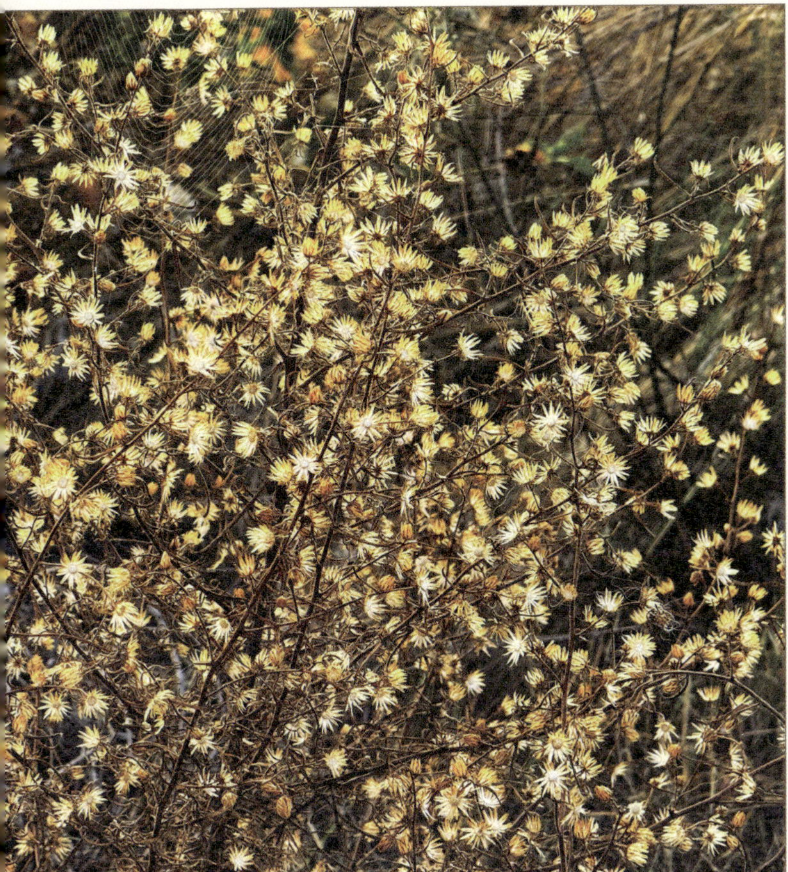

Part 1
慈：給予眾生安樂

把慈悲形象化，付諸具體的行動。

——《靜思語·第一集》

Let us actualize compassion through concrete actions.

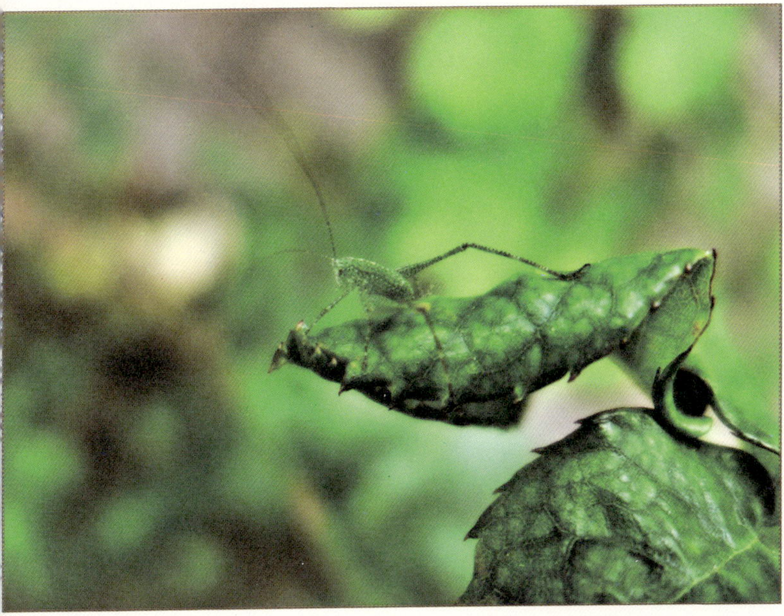

Part 1
慈：給予眾生安樂

眞正的妙法是：以智慧流露出來的方法；眞正的慈悲是：以智慧的力量去推動濟世志業的心願。

——《靜思語・第一集》

True, wondrous Dharma flows out of wisdom. Through the power of wisdom, we can fulfill our aspiration to benefit the world. This is true compassion.

Part 1

慈：給予眾生安樂

佛陀在人間,無非是要教導眾生自覺與佛同等的智慧,也要教導眾生與佛有同樣的自性,都能修持慈悲與智慧。

——《靜思語·第一集》

The Buddha came to this world to guide us to awaken our wisdom and to show us that we have the same intrinsic nature as his. Like him, we can also cultivate compassion and wisdom.

Part 1
慈：給予眾生安樂

光有慈悲而缺少智慧，有時也會衍生弊病。例如社會上常有善心人士被騙，如此慈悲不僅未能達到行善的目的，反而助長了騙徒的惡行。所以，我們要以智慧發揮慈悲，才是真正的善。

——《靜思語・第一集》

If you have compassion but lack wisdom, problems may arise. For instance, kindhearted people are often swindled by others. When this happens, not only is compassion not helpful to achieving the goal of doing good deeds, it has enabled the evil deeds of the swindlers. Therefore, we must exercise compassion with wisdom in order to truly accomplish goodness.

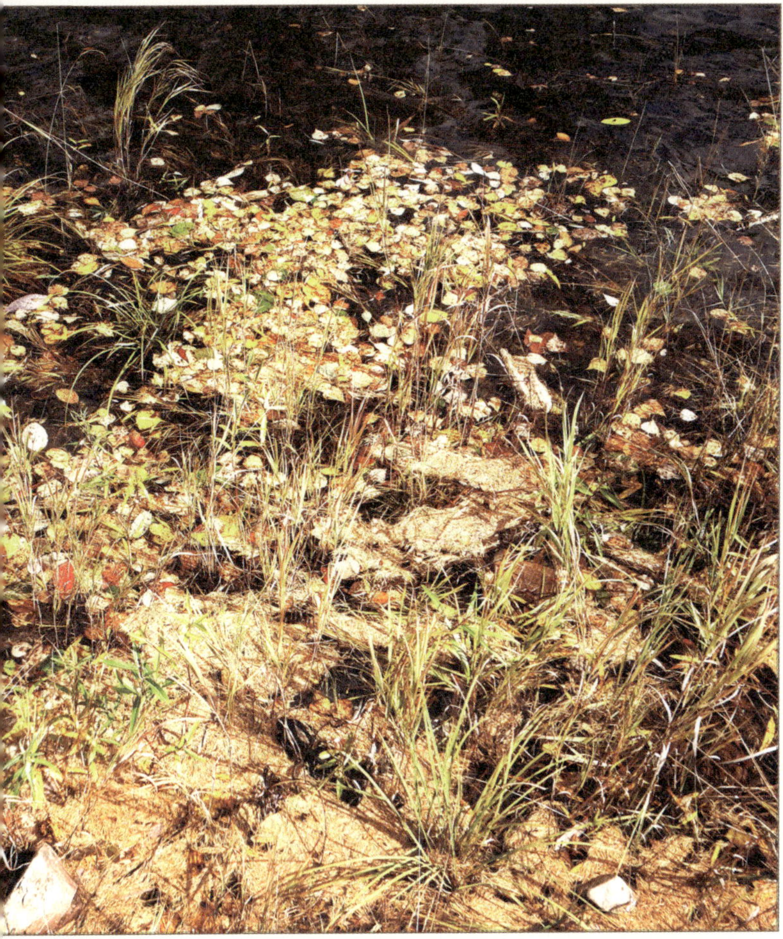

Part 1
慈：給予眾生安樂

人人本具一顆菩薩心，也具有和菩薩同等的精神與力量，此力量即慈悲與智慧的力量，它恆藏在人人內心的本性。

——《靜思語・第二集》

Everyone innately has the spirit and strength of a Bodhisattva, a power that comes from compassion and wisdom, which are part of our intrinsic Buddha-nature.

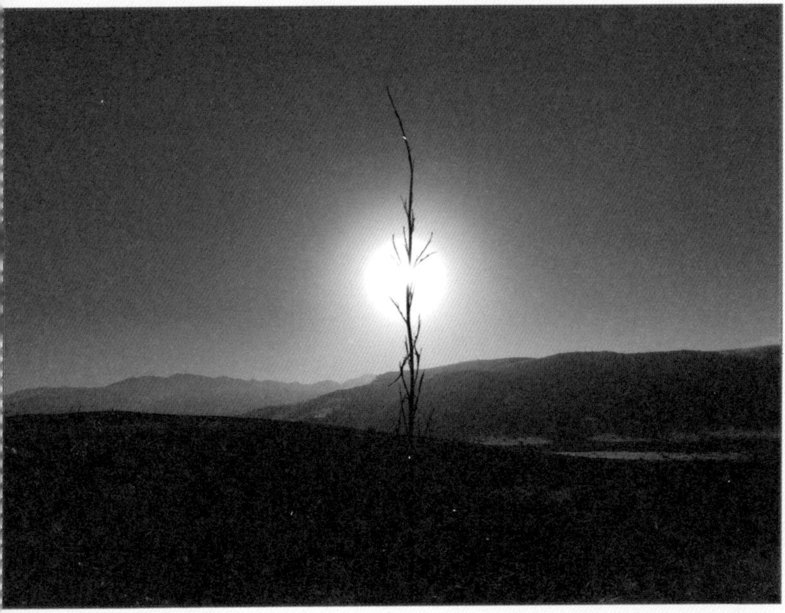

Part 1
慈：給予眾生安樂

菩薩行者心懷慈悲，常起利益眾生的念頭，無論到任何地方，心都無畏懼。因此，若能做到以愛待人、以慈對人，則不惹人怨，亦能結好緣。

——《靜思語‧第二集》

Bodhisattva-practitioners are compassionate. They always strive to benefit all beings. Thus, no matter what, they are never afraid. By treating others with love and kindness, they never offend others and always form good affinities.

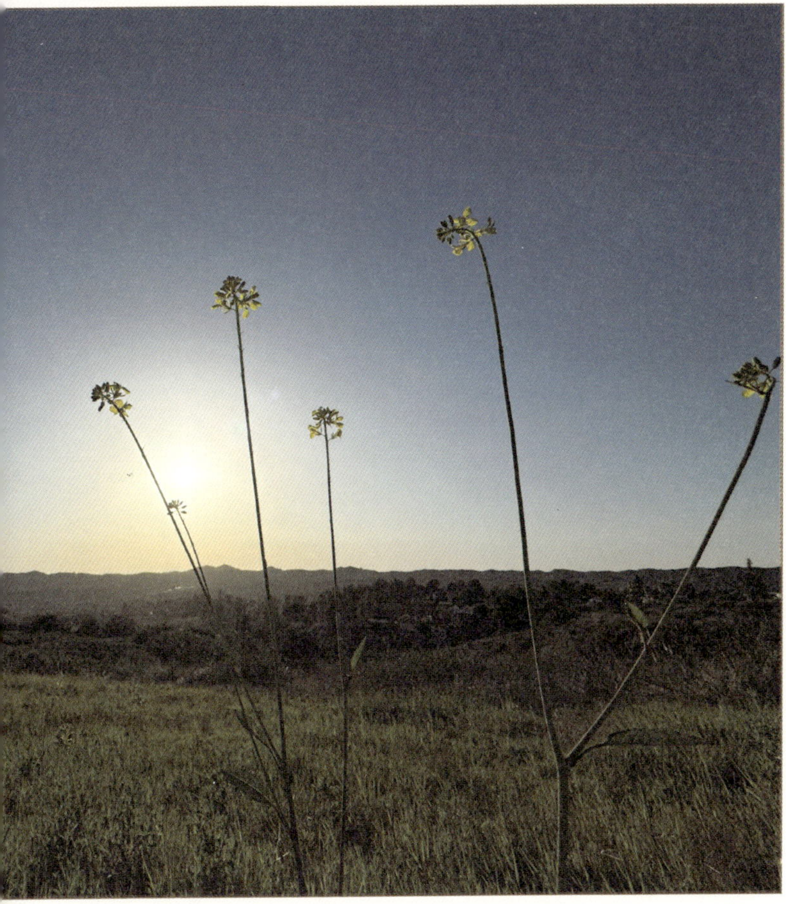

Part 1
慈:給予眾生安樂

學佛,最重要的是培養慈悲心。若失去了慈悲心,就是失去佛教的精神。

——《靜思語·第二集》

As Buddhist practitioners, it is most important to cultivate compassion. Without compassion, we are missing the spirit of the Buddha's teachings.

Part 1
慈:給予眾生安樂

時時保持快樂的心境,把快樂的氣氛散布給四周的人,此即「慈」;眾生有苦難能及時爲其拔除,此即「悲」。

——《靜思語・第二集》

Loving-kindness means always being happy and sharing that happiness with everyone. Compassion means promptly bringing relief to those who are suffering.

以愛待人、以慈對人,則不惹人怨,亦能結好緣。
　　　　　　——《靜思小語 1》

When we treat others with love and compassion, we will not stir up ill feelings, and we will be able to form good relationships with others.

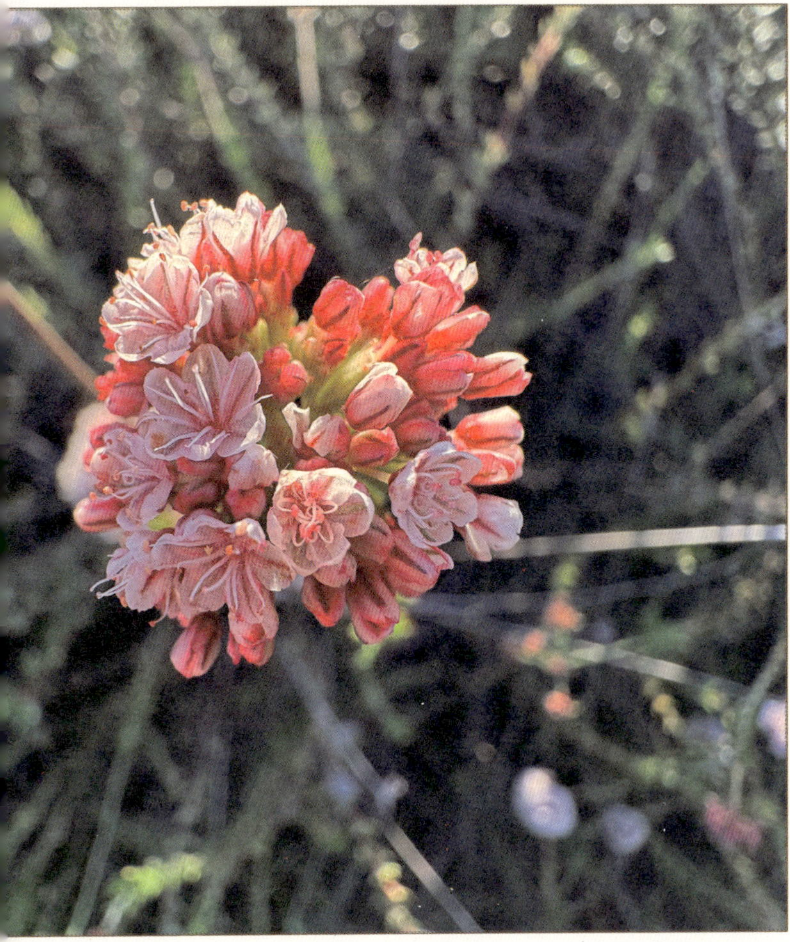

Part 1
慈：給予眾生安樂

不要輕視己靈,我們與佛有同等的智慧、同等的慈悲大愛,佛能我亦能。

——《靜思語・第二集》

We should not look down on ourselves, for we have the same wisdom, compassion, and great love as the Buddha. What the Buddha can do, we can also accomplish.

Part 1
慈：給予眾生安樂

有慈悲心的人,就會有柔和的風度;
慈悲柔和可以化解人的煩惱。

——《靜思語·第二集》

With compassion comes a gentle demeanor. With compassion and gentleness, we can help people resolve their worries.

Part 1
慈：給予眾生安樂

在苦惱的眾生中，能起勇猛精進心、慈悲心、喜捨心去救助苦難的人，才能獲得心靈上的快樂和永恆的解脫。

——《靜思語・第二集》

By relieving sentient beings from suffering with loving-kindness, compassion, joy, and equanimity, we can obtain spiritual happiness and everlasting liberation.

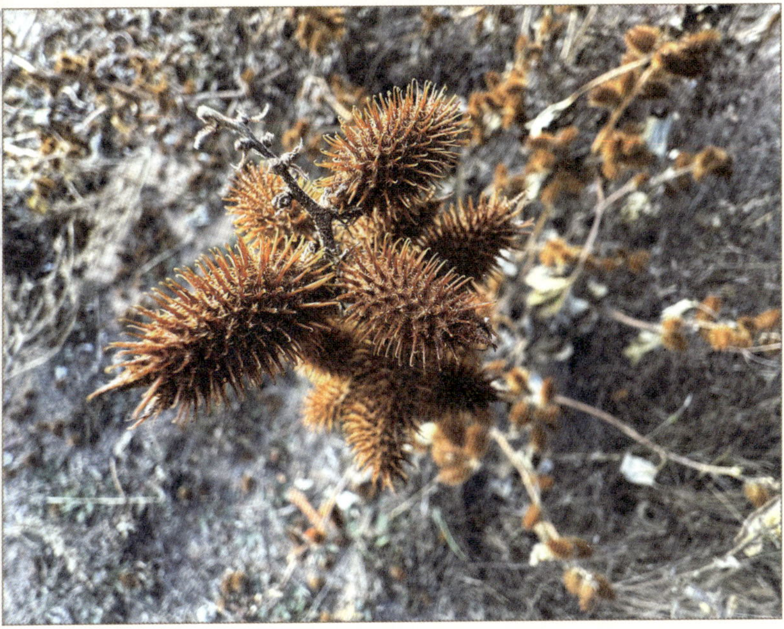

Part 1
慈：給予眾生安樂

願我們的慈悲心永恆地散布到每一角落,使眾生如沐浴在溫和明亮的月光下,得到真正的清涼快樂!

——《靜思語・第二集》

May our compassion reach every corner of the world. May it bathe sentient beings in happiness like the soft and gentle touch of moonlight.

Part 1
慈：給予眾生安樂

把貪念轉爲滿足,把滿足化作慈悲;如此,不但能自我滿足,還可發揮「用慈施悲」的愛心。

——《靜思語・第二集》

We should turn greed into contentment, and contentment into compassion. Then, not only will we be content with ourselves, we will tap into the love in our hearts to help others.

Part 1
慈：給予眾生安樂

仁慈、善良的人，以樂人之樂為樂、利人之利為利，此即真正的智慧；如果以利己之利為利，則只是聰明而非智慧。

——《靜思語‧第二集》

People who are good and kind feel happy when others are happy, and do things that benefit others. This is true wisdom. If people only do things that benefit themselves, they may be clever but not wise.

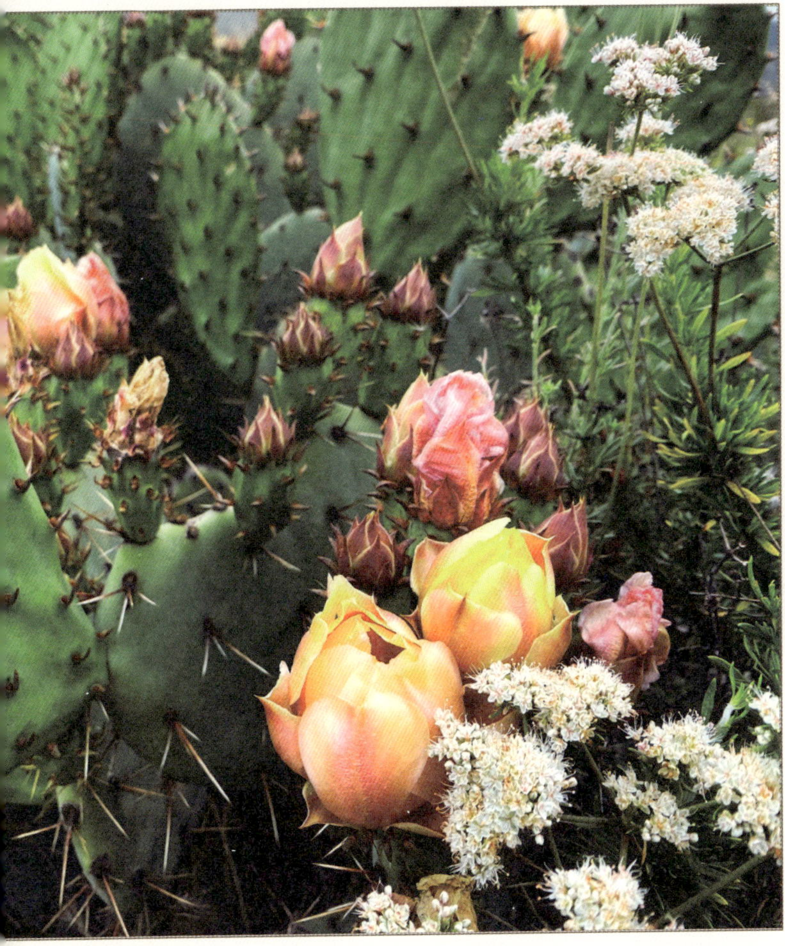

Part 1
慈：給予眾生安樂

「慈悲」和「博愛」有何不同？「慈悲」的含義較寬廣，慈遍無緣，悲至同體，於蠢動含靈，無微不至；而「博愛」卻只限於人類。

——《靜思語・第二集》

What is the difference between the Buddhist concept of compassion and people's ordinary concept of love?

The difference is that compassion is all-encompassing and limitless. As Buddhists, we love everything that lives, even the tiniest mosquito or worm, whereas in most cases, ordinary concepts of love extend only to human beings.

Part 1
慈：給予眾生安樂

轉一念心，為別人設想；忍一時氣，以悲智任事，則人事圓滿。

——《靜思語・孝為人本》

By shifting our perspective, we can put ourselves in others' shoes. By controlling our temper and handling matters with compassion and wisdom, we can attain satisfactory results and preserve harmonious relationships.

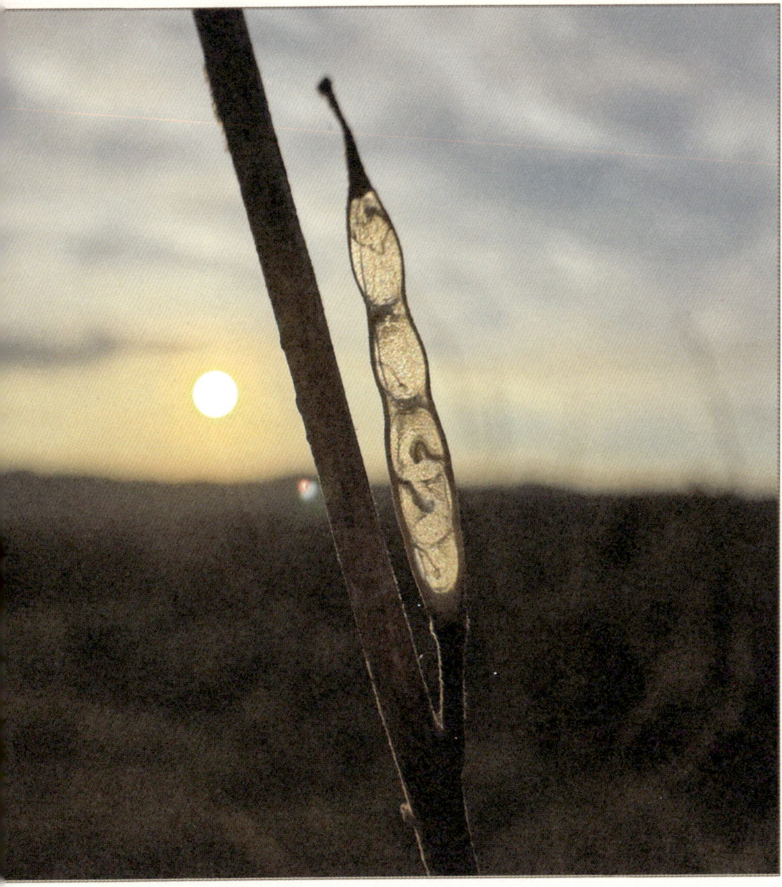

Part 1
慈：給予眾生安樂

浙江象山沿岸小漁港

大悲以身爲天下，苦人之苦；大智以身爲天下，樂人之樂；大愛以恆善救人，常無棄人；常存善念救物命，故無棄物。

——《靜思語‧孝為人本》

People with great compassion care for the world as if caring for themselves; they feel the pain of those who suffer. People with great wisdom also care for the world as if caring for themselves; they rejoice at the happiness of others. People with great love help others with unending kindness and never give up on anyone. With kind thoughts, they always find new uses for cast-offs and never give up on anything usable.

Part 1
慈：給予眾生安樂

世上的一草一木看來都好親切，樹上有青青的毛毛蟲，石頭上有如毫芒般的小蜘蛛以及其他的小蟲；小生命都很有靈性，都能和樂共處，互不相礙，人與人之間，不也該像牠們一樣嗎？

——《靜思語‧孝為人本》

Every blade of grass and every tree in the world is endearing. There are green caterpillars in the trees as well as tiny spiders and bugs crawling about on the rocks. Every little creature is sentient and they all coexist peacefully without disturbing one another. Should we not be like them in our interpersonal relationships?

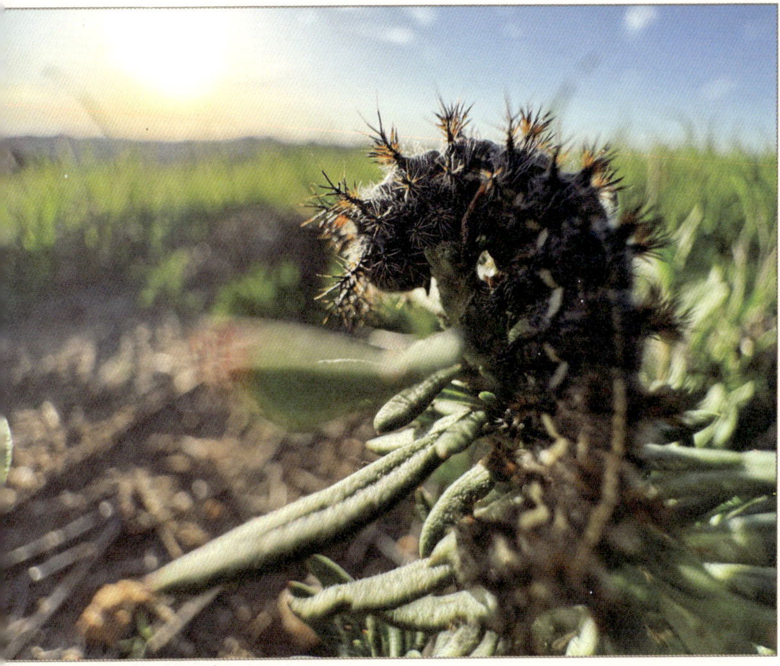

Part 1
慈：給予眾生安樂

菩薩心，永存春陽在內心，大愛伸向苦難人，陽光透進人心中，為人間帶來春天的氣息。

——《靜思語・孝為人本》

Bodhisattvas always carry the sunshine of spring within them. They help people in need with great love, shine their light into their hearts, and bring an air of spring to the world.

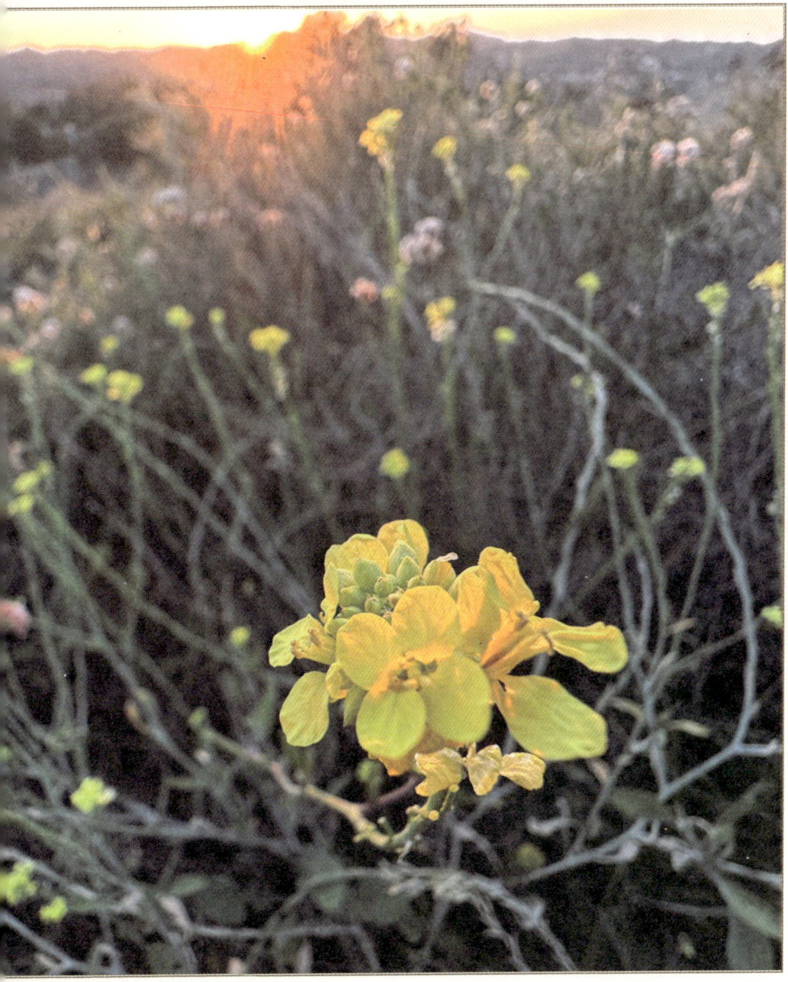

Part 1
慈：給予眾生安樂

有形的建築物蓋得再高都會被超越，無形的心靈境界則是自修自得；當不斷自我超越直至「慈悲等觀」的境界，如佛菩薩不起分別心，能平等看待眾生、度化眾生。

——《靜思語・孝為人本》

No matter how tall a building is, a higher one will always be built. When it comes to our state of mind, which is intangible, we reap what we sow. We should keep surpassing ourselves until we can treat everything equally with compassion. If we can be like Buddhas and Bodhisattvas in not differentiating between beings, then we will be able to treat all beings equally as well as to transform and save them.

Part 1
慈：給予眾生安樂

以菩薩的智慧,膚慰眾生的苦難,同時撒播愛的種子,使他們也體會到助人的歡喜,去除心中的埋怨,此即慈善人文。

——《靜思語・孝為人本》

We should exercise the wisdom of a Bodhisattva to comfort suffering beings. At the same time, we should spread the seeds of love so that they will understand the joy of helping people and eliminate the complaints in their hearts. This is the humanistic culture of charity.

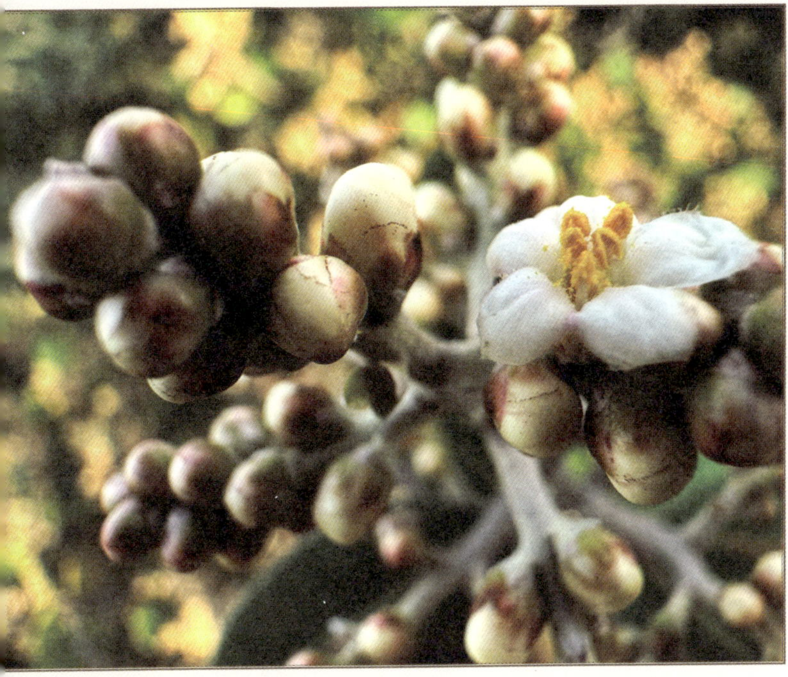

Part 1
慈：給予眾生安樂

人間菩薩如大地農夫，平常時走入片片心田撒播愛的種子，帶動有規則秩序的生活；非常時就做後援救災工作，號召人人付出愛的能量，有條不紊地恢復家園。

——《靜思語·孝為人本》

Living Bodhisattvas are like farmers. In times of peace, they reach into people's hearts to spread seeds of love, encouraging them to live an orderly life. In times of emergency, they support disaster relief efforts, calling on everyone to pool their power of love to methodically rebuild their homes.

洛杉磯附近山區

Part 1
慈：給予眾生安樂

人與人之間的互動要「覺有情」——覺悟的有情,而非「絕有情」——拒絕有情;對己嚴格自律守規則,帶人以寬以純以慈悲,在和氣互愛中展現溫馨的朝氣與道氣。

——《靜思語・孝為人本》

When we interact with people, we need to be enlightened and compassionate. We should be stern with ourselves, but forgiving and compassionate toward others, and demonstrate a warm vigor and spirit of cultivation in harmonious and loving relationships.

Part 1
慈:給予眾生安樂

以慈悲開心門,包容無量人成就好因緣;用智慧啟善念,接引有緣人同修大願行。

——《靜思語・孝為人本》

We must open our hearts with compassion and accommodate countless others to form good relationships. We must give rise to kind thoughts wisely and invite like-minded people to cultivate together and carry out great vows.

Part 1
慈：給予眾生安樂

無私的愛，如不可或缺的清水，
滋潤人人乾涸的心田。

——《靜思語・孝為人本》

Selfless love is as indispensable as clean water. It nurtures our dry and hardened hearts.

81

Part 1
慈:給予眾生安樂

付出,在於真誠的心與溫言軟語的表達。

──《靜思語‧孝為人本》

We should give warmly with a sincere heart and gentle words.

Part 1

慈：給予眾生安樂

要看清人生的道理——以布施心轉慳貪，以慈悲心轉瞋恚，以智慧心轉愚癡。

——《靜思語・第三集》

Understand the truth of life—turn greed into generosity, hate into compassion, and ignorance into wisdom.

Part 1
慈：給予眾生安樂

以智慧行慈悲路,才不會差之毫釐,失之千里。

——《靜思語·第三集》

Use wisdom to guide one's compassion, and one will stay true to the path.

洛杉磯近郊空拍

Part 1
慈：給予眾生安樂

愛心不分遠近,慈悲沒有敵對和親愛。

——《靜思語・第三集》

Love is not bound by distance; compassion is free from aversion and passion.

Part 1
慈：給予眾生安樂

慈悲心要如天地寬、日月明。
　　　　——《靜思語·第三集》

A compassionate heart should be as broad as the sky and as bright as the sun and moon.

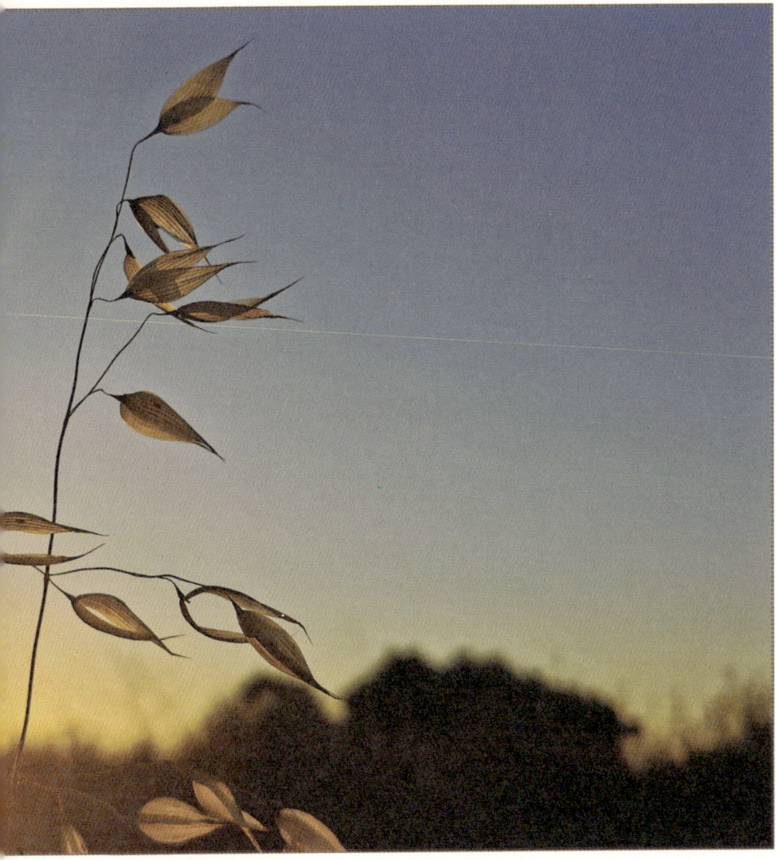

Part 1
慈：給予眾生安樂

對每件事、每個人都感恩，就能化貪心為慈悲心。

——《靜思語・第三集》

Keep gratitude in mind, and greed shall give way to compassion.

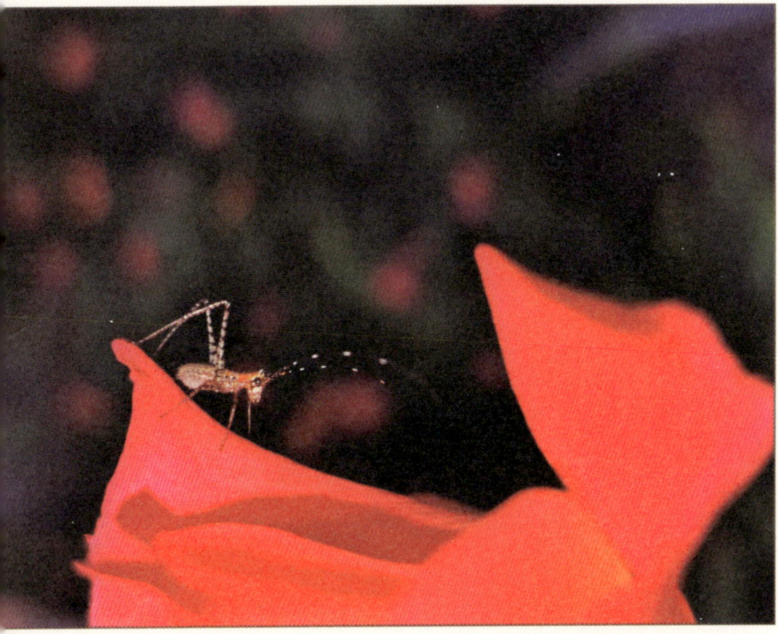

Part 1
慈：給予眾生安樂

開啟心胸,才能發揮無量的慈悲,獲致真正的智慧與功德。

——《靜思語·第三集》

Only by opening one's heart can one give with great compassion and gain true wisdom and virtue.

Part 1
慈：給予眾生安樂

以大慈悲心實踐大愛，以大智慧力超越煩惱。

——《靜思語‧第三集》

Great love manifests itself through practicing great compassion; wisdom manifests itself through transcending worries.

內蒙古額爾古納市

Part 1
慈：給予眾生安樂

無悔無怨,見證慈悲;無憂無求,體證喜捨。

——《靜思語‧第三集》

Kindness and compassion bear neither regret nor complaint; and equanimity is free of want and worry.

Part 1

慈:給予眾生安樂

洛杉磯附近山區

感恩是智慧,付出是慈悲。

——《靜思語·第三集》

Gratitude is wisdom; giving is compassion.

Part 1
慈：給予眾生安樂

談「利」要談天下利；說「愛」要說眾生愛。

——《靜思語・第三集》

When discussing "benefit," one must talk about the benefit for the world. When discussing "love," one must talk about the love for all living beings.

103

Part 1
慈：給予眾生安樂

所謂「布施」不完全指財物的布施，
溫言慧語或伸手助人，都是布施。

——《靜思語・十在心路・壹》

The practice of giving (dāna in sanskrit) does not only refer to the giving of the material things; gentle, kind words, or lending a helping hands are all forms of giving.

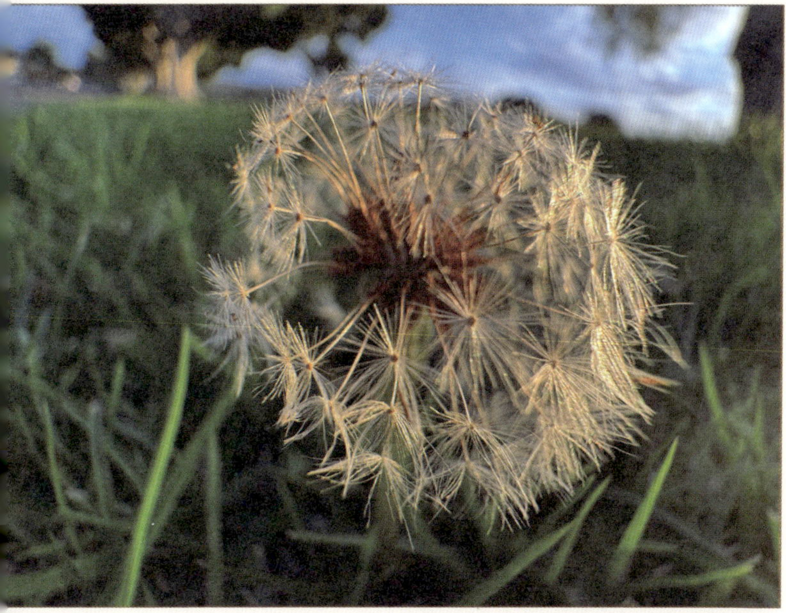

Part 1

慈:給予眾生安樂

心,寬廣如浩瀚虛空,普愛一切;身,包容如大地之母,滋養萬物。

——《靜思語·十在心路·伍》

Our hearts should be as vast as the boundless universe, embracing all with love. Our bodies should be all-encompassing like Mother Earth, nurturing all living beings.

Part 1
慈:給予眾生安樂

天下多災難,要恆持清淨心,時時戒慎、念念虔誠、步步精進,救人心且救大地。

——《靜思語·十在心路·伍》

In a world fraught with disasters, we must maintain a pure heart and be vigilant. Be sincere in every thought. With every step we take, we must diligently advance. In doing so, we are saving people's hearts and saving the Earth.

Part 1
慈：給予眾生安樂

快樂的根源不是金錢財富，而是幫助人脫困脫苦所得的法喜。

——《靜思語‧十在心路‧捌》

The root of happiness does not lie in wealth or riches, but in the spiritual joy that arises from helping others escape hardship and suffering.

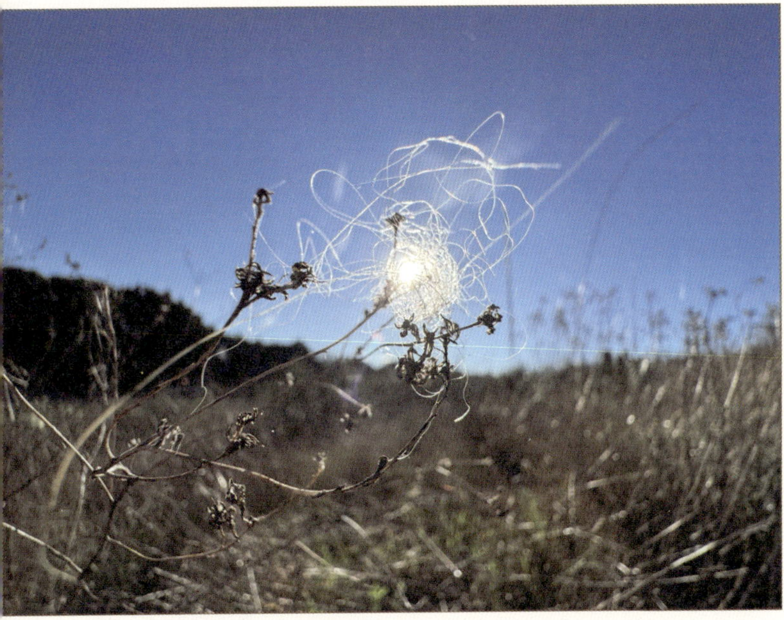

Part 1
慈：給予眾生安樂

不只幫助貧者生活脫貧，還要引導其心靈因有愛而富足。

——《靜思語・十在心路・捌》

It is not enough to help the poor rise from poverty; we must also guide their hearts to feel abundance through love.

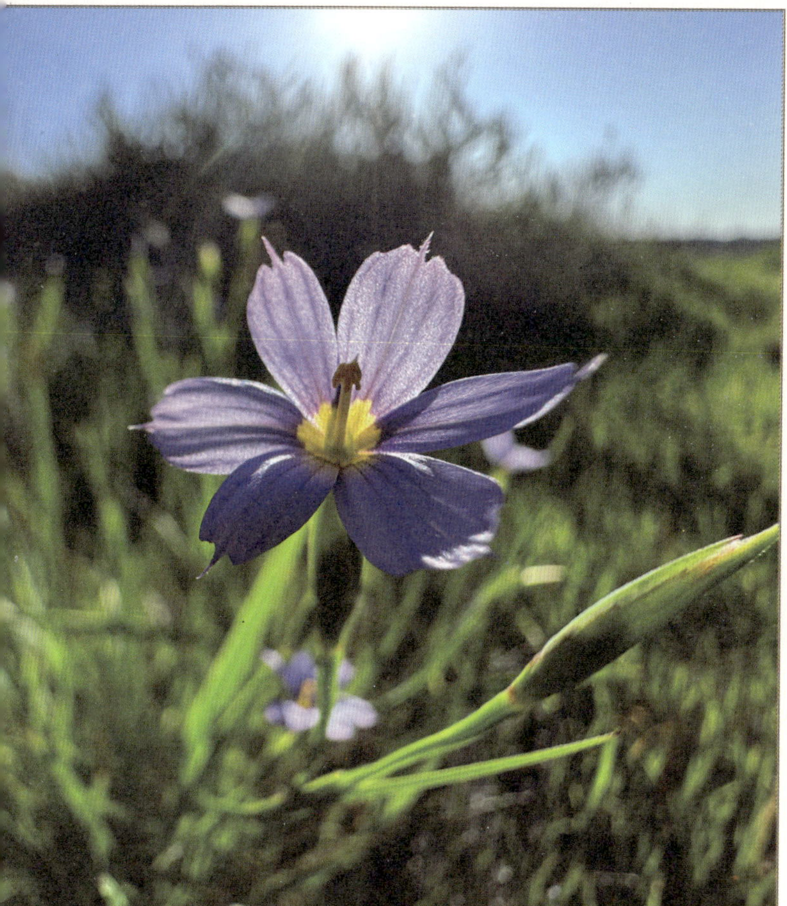

Part 1
慈：給予眾生安樂

引導苦難人身心都能自立，
才是徹底的救助。

——《靜思語‧十在心路‧捌》

Guiding those in hardship to achieve both physical and spiritual self-reliance is the most thorough way to provide aid.

Part 1
慈：給予眾生安樂

人與人之間，要互為善知識，以明鏡互照，時時淨化心地。

——《靜思語‧十在心路‧捌》

In our relationships with others, we should serve as virtuous friends to one another, reflecting our companions like clear mirrors and constantly purifying our hearts.

西藏纳木措

Part 1
慈：給予眾生安樂

提起平等心,愛護一切眾生;發揮同理心,救拔眾生苦難。

——《靜思語·十在心路·玖》

Let us cultivate a sense of equality and cherish all beings. Let us exercise empathy and alleviate the suffering of all beings.

Part 1

慈：給予眾生安樂

扶助苦難、撫平人心傷痛,在苦難地留下「愛足跡」。

——《靜思語・十在心路・玖》

We must help those who are suffering and soothe their wounded hearts, leaving footprints of love where once there was hardship.

Part 2
悲：拔除眾生痛苦

洛杉磯附近山區

悲即是同情心。能互相寬諒、容忍,表現一分寬心、愛心,即是悲心。最幸福的人生,就是能寬容與悲憫一切眾生的人生。

——《靜思語·第一集》

A heart of compassion is one that sympathizes and empathizes with others, one that is forgiving and patient. Acting from an open and loving heart shows a heart of compassion in action. Those who are able to forgive and accommodate all living beings with a compassionate heart lead the most blessed lives.

Part 2
悲：拔除眾生痛苦

眾生雖與我非親非故，但是他的苦就是我的苦，他的痛就是我的痛。苦在他的身，憂在我的心；傷在他的身，痛在我的心。這就是「同體大悲」。

——《靜思語・第一集》

Although others are not related to me, their hardships are my hardships, their pain my pain. The hardships may be happening to others, but they are of concern to me. When others hurt, I hurt as well. This is universal compassion, or great compassion for all.

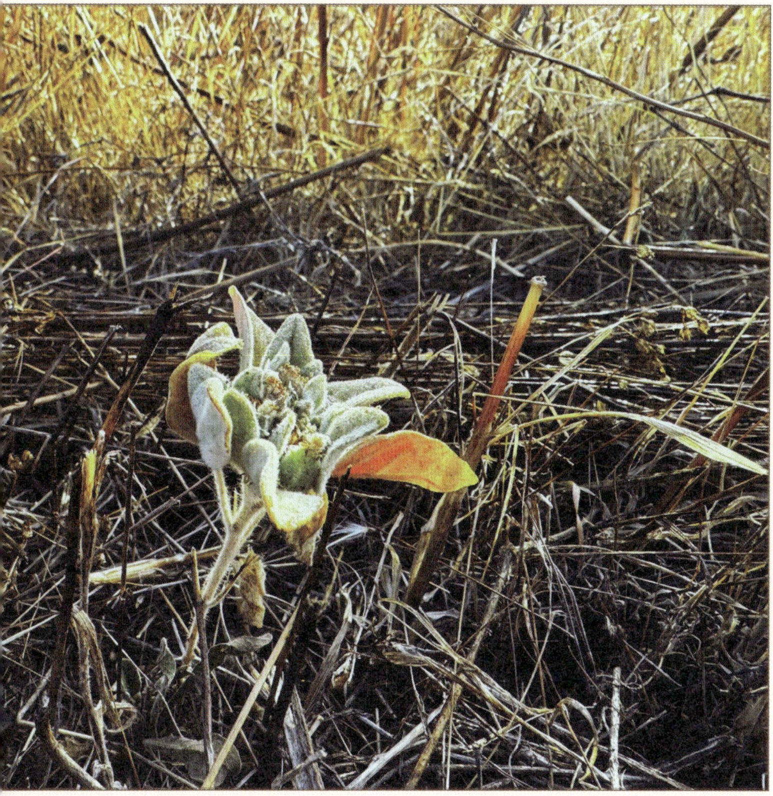

Part 2
悲：拔除眾生痛苦

要慈眼視眾生，把無形化作有形，把理論化成行動，時時刻刻拿出一分「我們不去救他，誰去救他」的大慈大悲濟助精神，能如此，塵世亦可成爲淨土。

——《靜思語‧第一集》

We should regard others with a compassionate heart and give form to the abstract by turning ideals into action. At every moment, we should bring forth the compassionate thought, "If we don't save them, who will?" If we can do this, even this impure world can become a pure land.

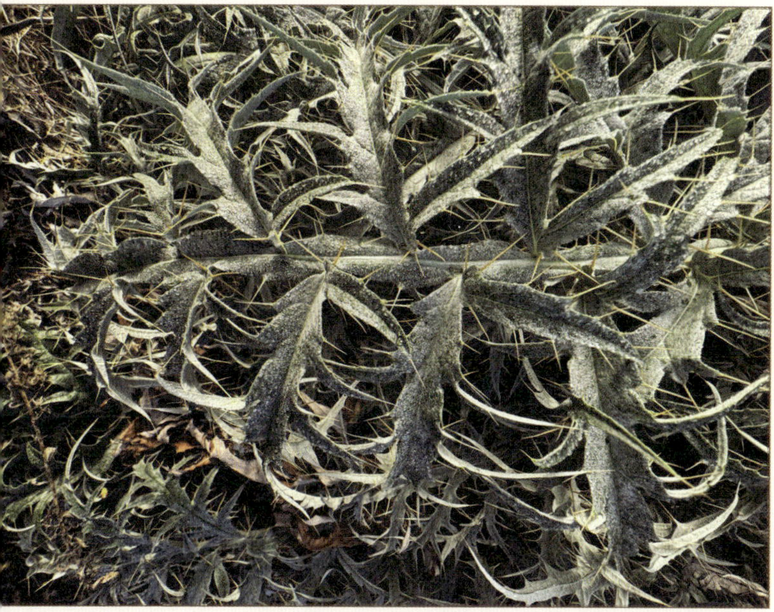

Part 2
悲：拔除眾生痛苦

慈悲是救世的泉源,但無智不成大悲。有智慧才能發揮無窮的毅力與慈悲,此即佛法中的「悲智雙運」。

——《靜思語·第一集》

Compassion is the wellspring for saving the world, but without wisdom, we cannot attain great compassion. Only with wisdom can we exercise limitless perseverance and compassion. This is the meaning of practicing both compassion and wisdom as taught by the Buddha.

Part 2
悲:拔除眾生痛苦

能救人的人就叫做菩薩。把握一日的付出,即是一日的菩薩。

——《靜思語·第一集》

Those who can help others are called bodhisattvas; if we seize this day to help others, then today we are bodhisattvas.

西藏納木措

Part 2
悲：拔除眾生痛苦

菩薩精神永遠融入眾生的精神。要讓菩薩精神永遠存在這個世界，不能只有理論，必須有實質的表現；慈悲與願力是理論，服務眾生的工作是實質的表現。我們要把無形的慈悲化為有形、堅固、永遠的工作。

——《靜思語・第一集》

The spirit of a Bodhisattva is always one with the spirits of living beings. For the spirit of the Bodhisattva to always remain in this world, we cannot depend on ideals alone. We must put them into action. Compassion and commitment are ideals, while the work of saving people takes practical action. We must turn formless compassion into concrete and sustainable deeds.

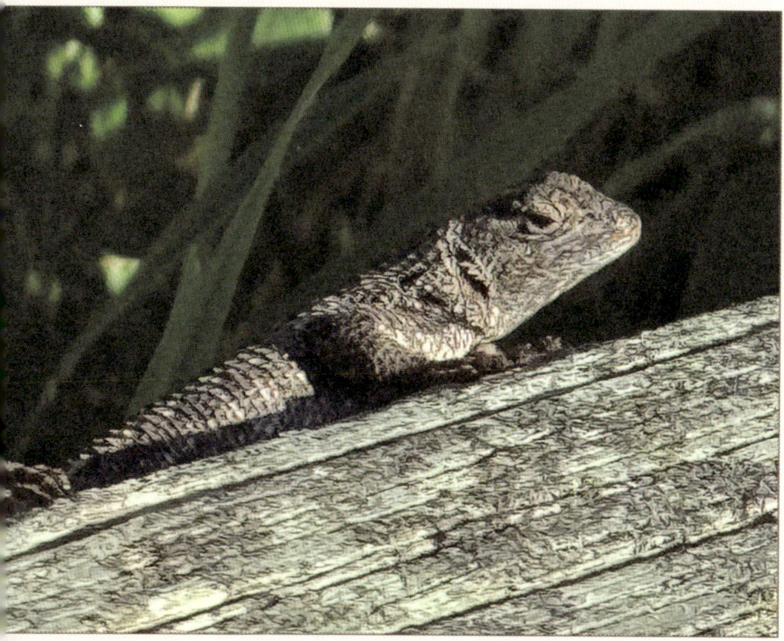

Part 2
悲：拔除眾生痛苦

要突破小範圍的愛，將愛心普及一切眾生，視眾生的苦痛如自己的苦痛，這才是佛教所倡導的愛。

——《靜思語・第二集》

We must transcend the limits of our personal feelings of love and regard the suffering of all beings as our own. This is the Buddha's spirit of love.

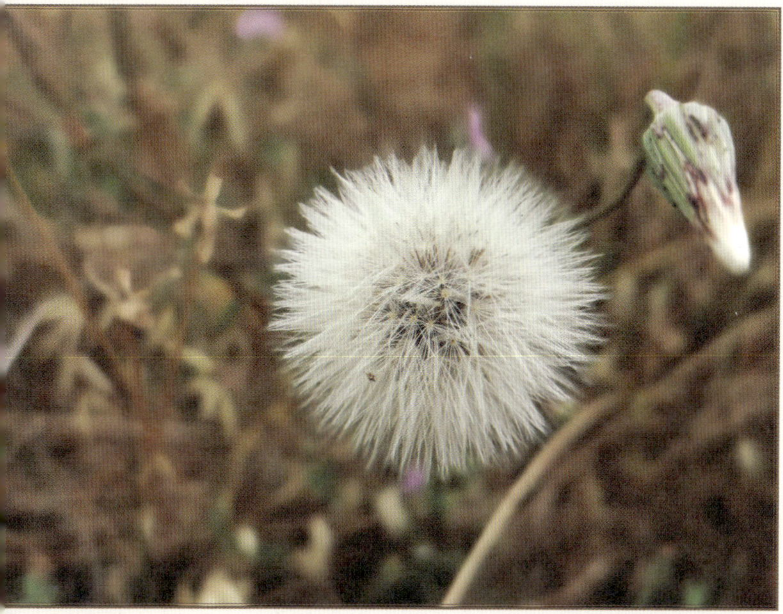

Part 2
悲:拔除眾生痛苦

以佛陀普愛天下眾生之心爲己心。佛陀能爲一切眾生犧牲，我們也能爲濟助眾生的志業不惜辛勞付出。

——《靜思語·第二集》

We should emulate the Buddha's universal love. The Buddha is able to dedicate himself to all living beings; we also have the ability to tirelessly devote ourselves to saving all beings.

Part 2
悲：拔除眾生痛苦

為了願心與歡喜心而服務人群的人，能不惜承擔重任，不畏辛苦地勇往直前！只要眾生能離苦得救，就滿心歡喜，別無所求。

——《靜思語·第二集》

When we serve others out of sincerity and joy, we will take on hard work without hesitation and courageously move forward in the face of adversity. So long as they are relieved of their suffering, we will be filled with joy; this is all we ask for.

Part 2
悲：拔除眾生痛苦

發揮內心溫暖的愛,不辭勞苦、不畏繁重、不計艱辛,但願膚慰苦難者的身心,這分關懷天下的開闊愛心,就是佛陀正法的教育。

——《靜思語・孝為人本》

Regardless of the hard work and difficulties we face, we should bring forth the warm love in our hearts to comfort both the minds and bodies of people in suffering. This profound love that cares for the whole world is what the Buddha's true Dharma aims to teach.

Part 2
悲：拔除眾生痛苦

菩薩以災為師，以天下災情為師、為道場，要珍惜可以付出的時機，因應災民的需求，在能力範圍內盡心力，儘量達到有求必應的程度。

——《靜思語・孝為人本》

Bodhisattvas learn from disasters; they regard disasters around the world as teachers and cultivation grounds. We must cherish the opportunities to serve others and meet the needs of disaster survivors to the best of our ability.

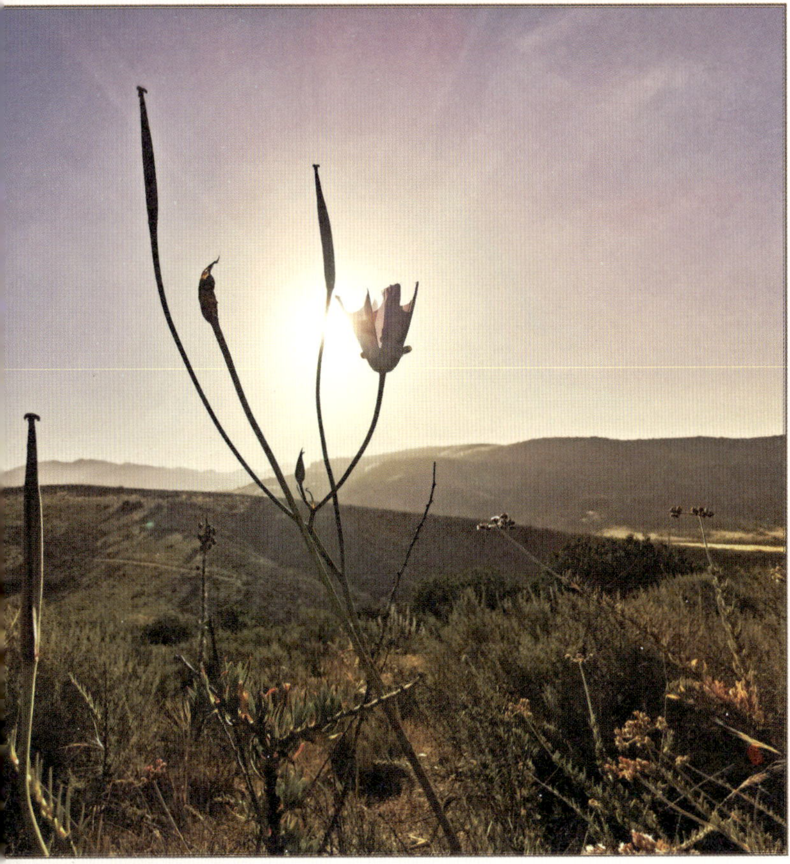

Part 2
悲：拔除眾生痛苦

人生最寶貴的是生命，最痛苦的是病痛，所以拔苦從拔除病苦開始。

——《靜思語·第三集》

The most precious possession is life, and the worst torment is illness. Ridding the world of suffering begins with ridding people of illness.

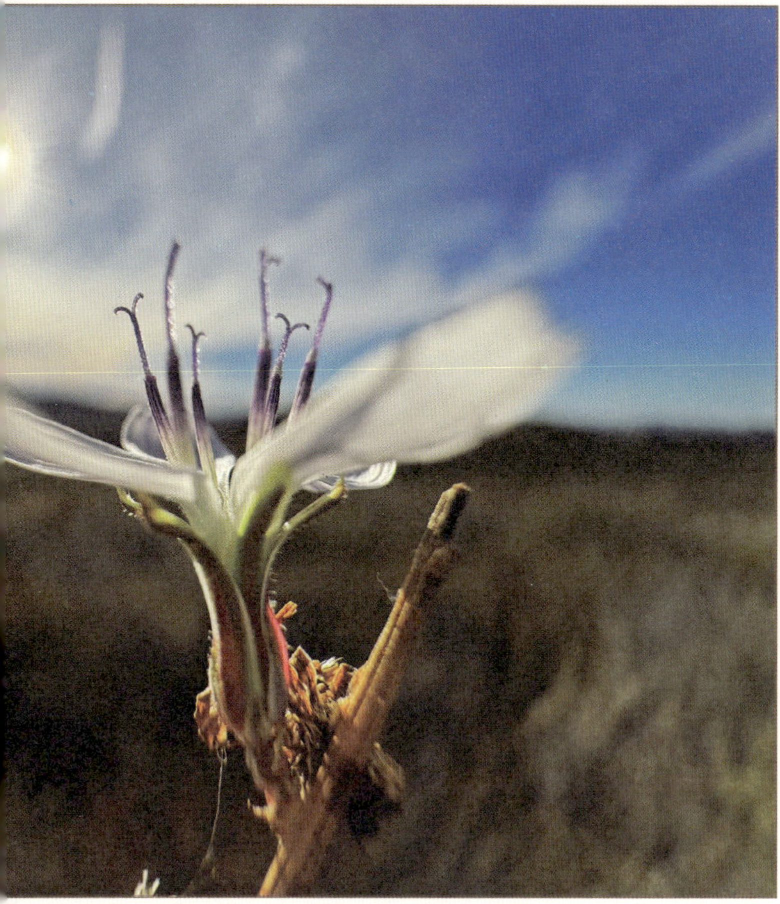

Part 2
悲：拔除眾生痛苦

教富,是啟發智慧;濟貧,是造福人群,也就是福慧雙修。

——《靜思語·第三集》

To educate the rich is to inspire wisdom; to help the poor is to benefit humanity. This is an example of cultivating both blessings and wisdom.

Part 2
悲：拔除眾生痛苦

給人安定、幸福，是大慈心的作用；用心救拔、度化是大悲心的發揮。

——《靜思語・第三集》

Loving-kindness helps to provide peace and happiness. Compassion serves to relieve suffering and benefit all living beings.

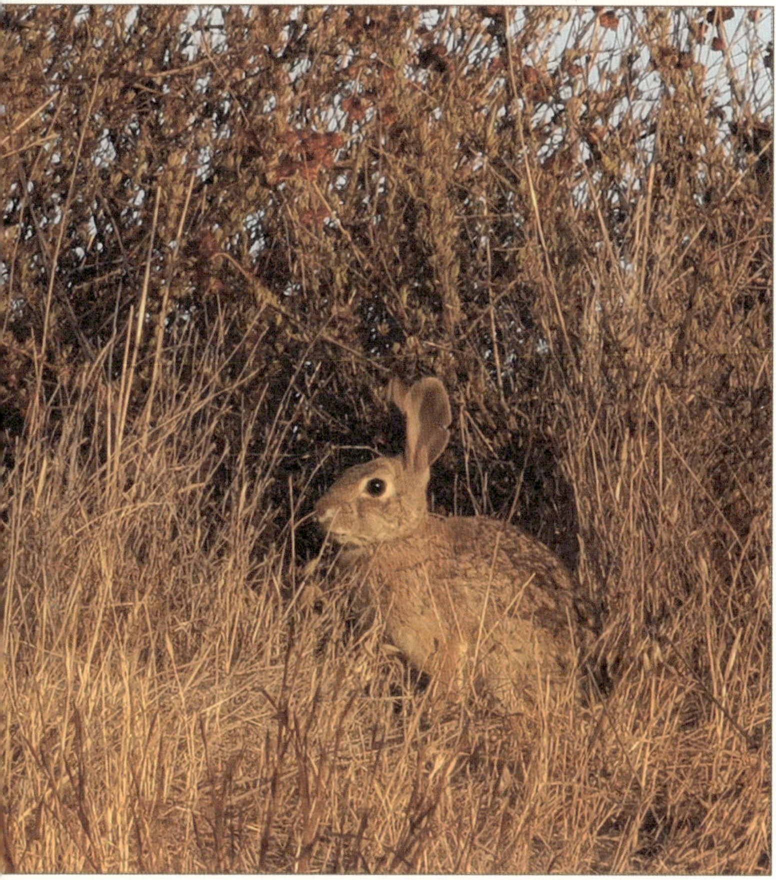

Part 2
悲：拔除眾生痛苦

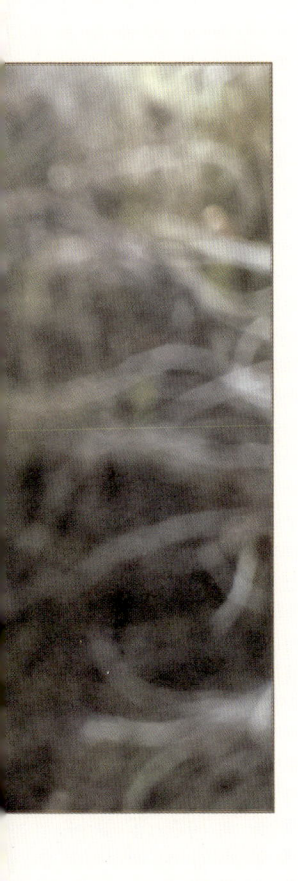

慈悲要從內心啟發,造福要用身體行動。

——《靜思語·第三集》

Compassion is inspired from within; blessings are created through action.

Part 2
悲：拔除眾生痛苦

長白山天池附近

有慈悲心,就是佛心;有愛心、
毅力,投入人群付出,是菩薩心
也是菩薩行。

——《靜思語・第三集》

With a heart of loving-kindness and compassion, we can realize the heart of the Buddha. When we walk among people to help others, we are walking the Bodhisattva Path with the heart of a bodhisattva.

Part 2
悲：拔除眾生痛苦

以「慈悲」爲原點,用「喜捨」爲推動力向前進步。
　　——《靜思語・第三集》

Start with loving-kindness and compassion, then move forward with the spirit of joy and selfless giving.

Part 2
悲:拔除眾生痛苦

素食可培養耐力、慈悲與智慧。
　　　　——《靜思語·第三集》

By practicing vegetarianism, we can cultivate perseverance, compassion, and wisdom.

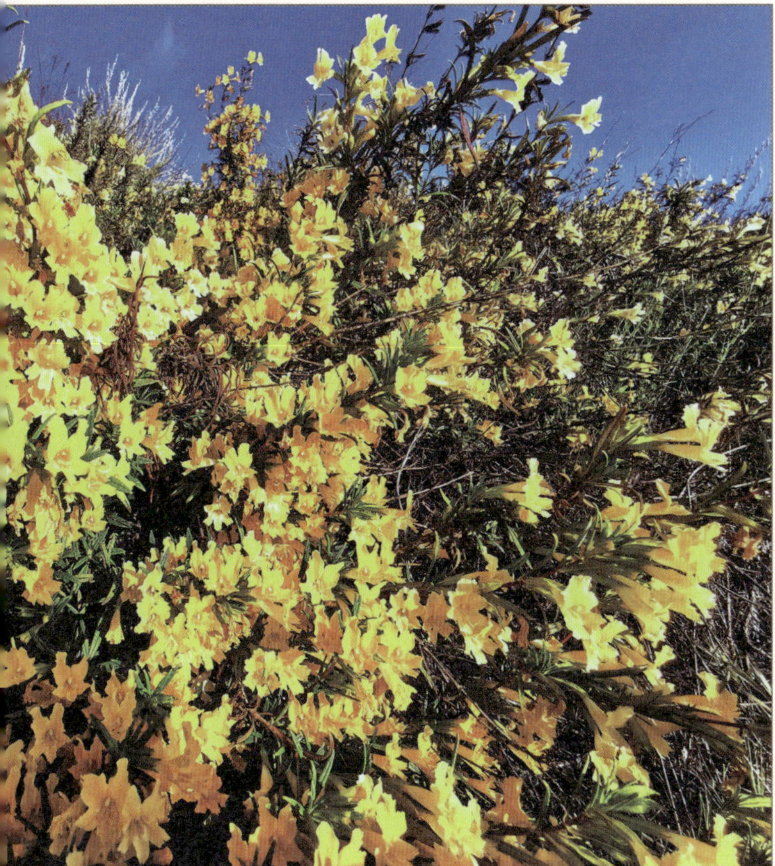

Part 2
悲：拔除眾生痛苦

洛杉磯附近山區

世間苦難,能啟動人的愛心;
只要有一分付出,就會有一分感動。

——《靜思語・第三集》

Misfortunes in the world have the power to inspire compassion. An act of giving has the power to touch people's hearts.

Part 2
悲：拔除眾生痛苦

長白山天池附近

真正的環保,是愛山、愛海,
愛惜一切萬物。

———《靜思語・第三集》

True environmental protection lies in loving the mountains and the oceans and in cherishing everything in this world.

Part 2
悲：拔除眾生痛苦

洛杉磯附近山區

疼愛大地,就是疼愛眾生。

——《靜思語・第三集》

To love our planet is to love all living beings.

Part 2
悲:拔除眾生痛苦

用感恩心疼惜大地萬物,生活簡單就無缺。
　　　　——《靜思語・第三集》

Love and cherish all of the Earth's resources with a heart of gratitude. Lead a simple life, then you will lack nothing.

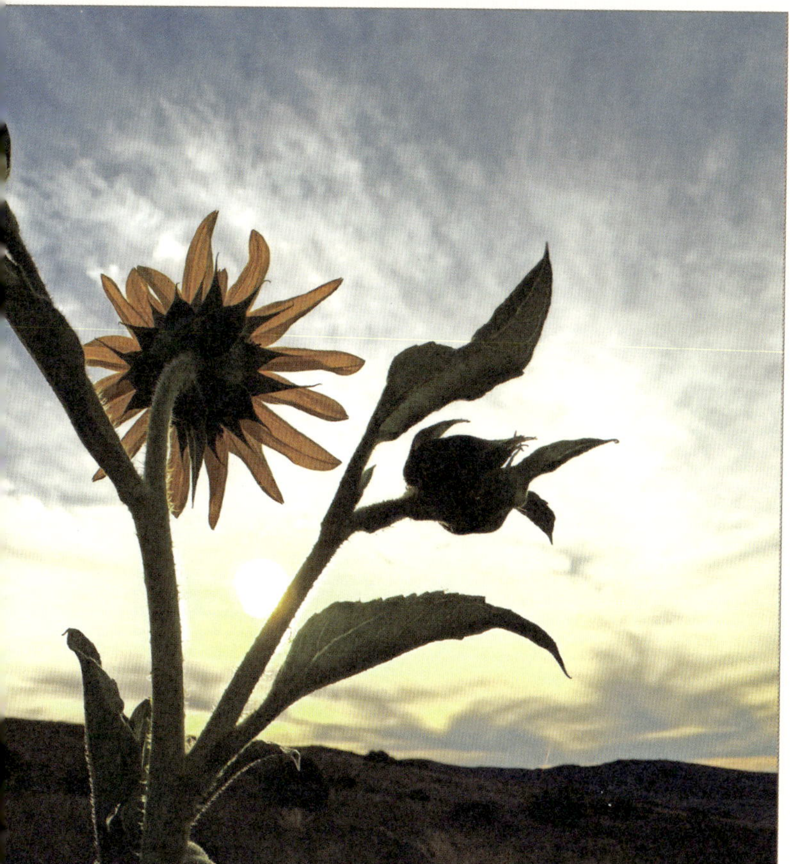

Part 2
悲：拔除眾生痛苦

慈悲不只用口說，而是要身體力行，走入人群付出。

——《靜思語・第三集》

Compassion is not only expressed through words; it is to be realized through service to humanity.

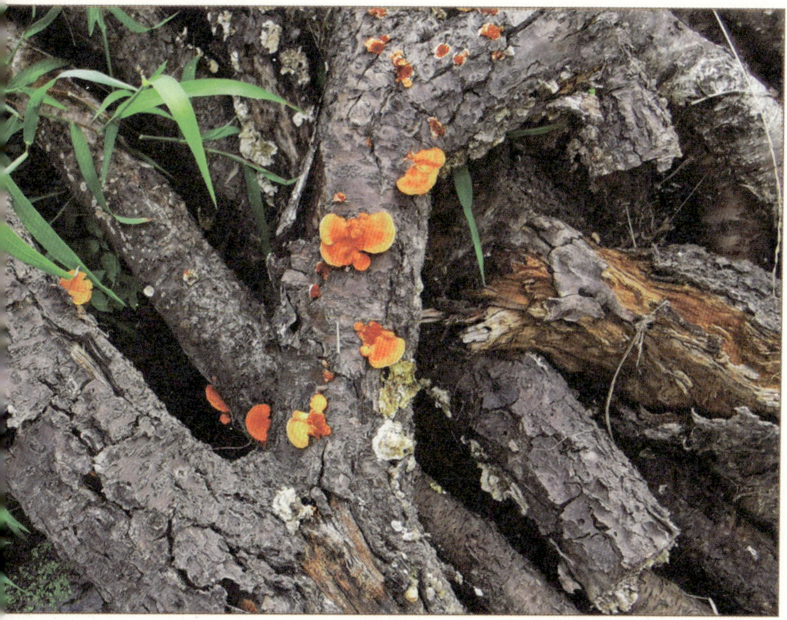

Part 2
悲：拔除眾生痛苦

力行菩薩道,不是求菩薩來感應;而是要去感應眾生之苦,無所求付出。

——《靜思語・十在心路・壹》

To truly walk the Bodhisattva Path, we should not seek blessings for ourselves, but rather care for the suffering, expecting nothing in return.

Part 2
悲：拔除眾生痛苦

慈善工作要有平等之愛，不分國界、種族和宗教，哪裡有需要，就到哪裡遍灑甘露。

——《靜思語・十在心路・壹》

Charitable work should embody universal love, transcending borders, races, and religions——bringing relief wherever there is need.

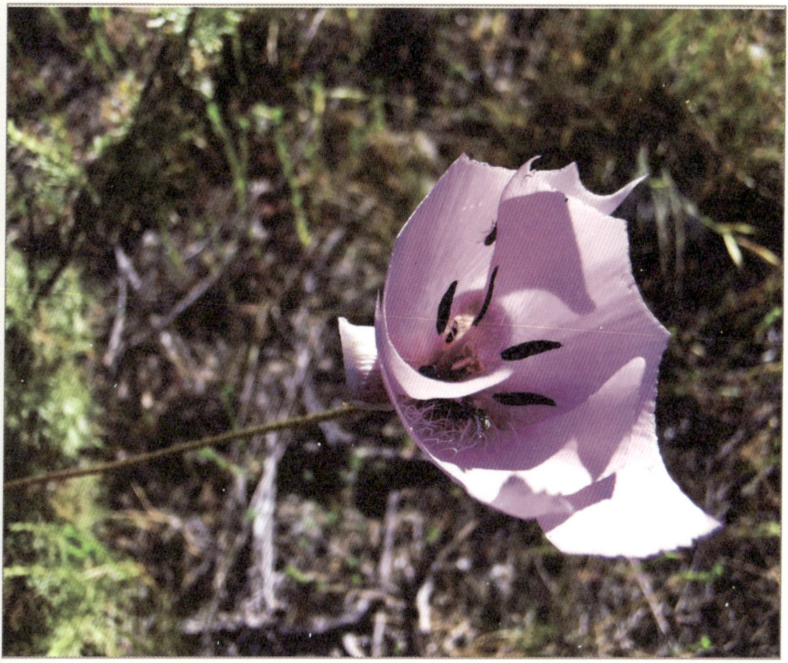

Part 2
悲：拔除眾生痛苦

將人間的苦難當成自己的使命,哪裡有災難,就能自動地動員。

——《靜思語・十在心路・壹》

When we treat the hardships of others as our own, then we can proactively respond and mobilize wherever disaster strikes.

Part 2
悲：拔除眾生痛苦

幫助苦難眾生得安樂，心靈自然清朗安詳。

——《靜思語・十在心路・壹》

By helping those in suffering attain peace and joy, our hearts will naturally become clear, bright, and serene.

洛杉磯附近山區

Part 2
悲：拔除眾生痛苦

智慧在人群中獲得，立願的悲心也自人群的苦難中激發。

——《靜思語・十在心路・壹》

As we interact with others, our wisdom grows. As we witness the suffering of others, we are inspired to make vows of compassion.

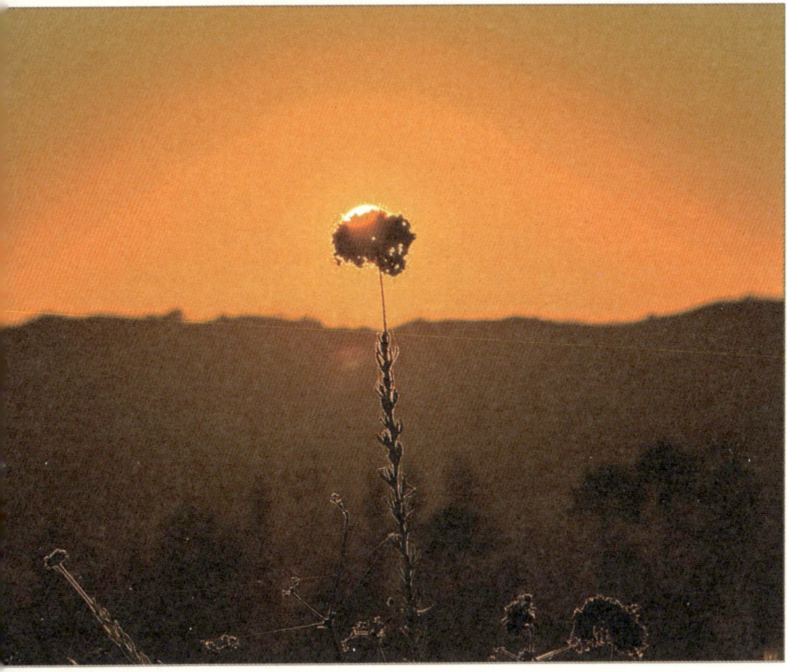

Part 2
悲：拔除眾生痛苦

受災的人可以因為感受到人情溫暖，而減輕受難的苦痛。

——《靜思語・十在心路・壹》

In receiving the warmth of human kindness, disaster survivors can find relief from suffering.

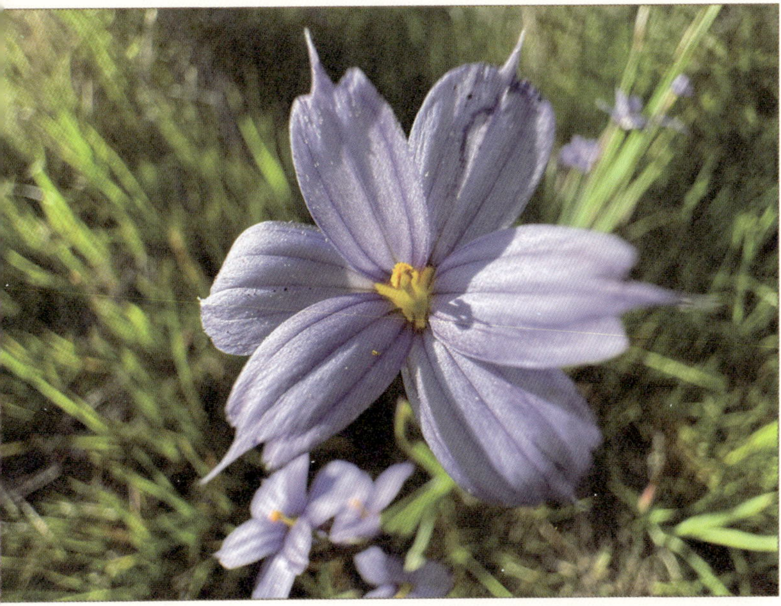

Part 2
悲：拔除眾生痛苦

深入人間疾苦,故能感同身受去拔苦予樂;明白苦來自何處,故能力行離苦得樂的解脫之道。

——《靜思語・十在心路・壹》

By immersing ourselves in the hardships of the world, we can empathize deeply and bring relief and joy to others. By realizing the root of suffering, we can diligently walk the path of liberation to relieve suffering and bring joy.

Part 2
悲：拔除眾生痛苦

對無緣無故的人,可以想辦法拔苦予樂;對生活周遭的人,怎可少寬懷、善解之心呢?

——《靜思語・十在心路・壹》

Knowing that we can find ways to ease the suffering of strangers and bring them joy, how can we not show more compassion and understanding toward those around us?

Part 2
悲:拔除眾生痛苦

在最困難的時刻、最需要幫助的地方,伸出援手助人離苦得樂,就是人生最尊貴的價值。

——《靜思語·十在心路·伍》

In the most challenging times and places where help is most needed, extending a hand to help others find relief and joy is the most noble value of life.

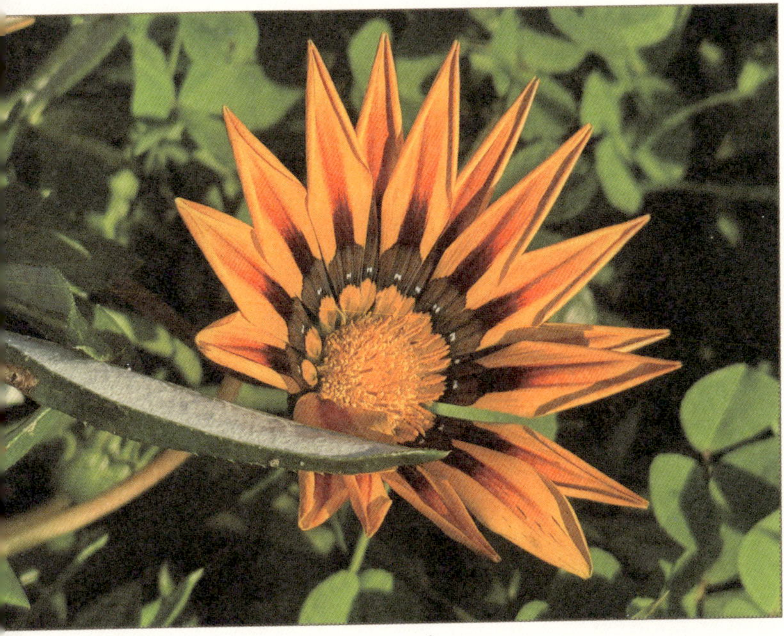

Part 2
悲：拔除眾生痛苦

一時災難,只要人人以愛伸援,就能帶來永恆希望。

——《靜思語‧十在心路‧伍》

At times of disaster, if everyone lends a helping hand with love, it can bring everlasting hope.

Part 2
悲：拔除眾生痛苦

苦難人需要大愛膚慰,有福人要用慈付出。

——《靜思語·十在心路·伍》

Those who suffer need the solace of great love, and those who are blessed must give with compassion.

Part 2
悲：拔除衆生痛苦

見苦知福,長養悲心;
放下私我,擁抱大我。

——《靜思語・十在心路・伍》

By witnessing suffering, we learn to appreciate our blessings and cultivate a heart of compassion; by letting go of selfishness, we embrace a greater self.

Part 2
悲：拔除眾生痛苦

腳要輕、手要柔,靠近、擁抱、膚慰身心受苦的人。

——《靜思語・十在心路・伍》

Walk with gentle steps and reach out with tender hands to approach, embrace, and soothe those who are suffering in body and mind.

Part 2
悲：拔除眾生痛苦

好緣纏綿是苦，惡緣相磨也是苦；唯有清淨光明的覺有情，才能拔苦予樂。

——《靜思語‧十在心路‧伍》

Bad relationships bring conflict, but good relationships may also become entangled and cause suffering. Only through the pure and radiant awakened love can we truly alleviate suffering and bring joy.

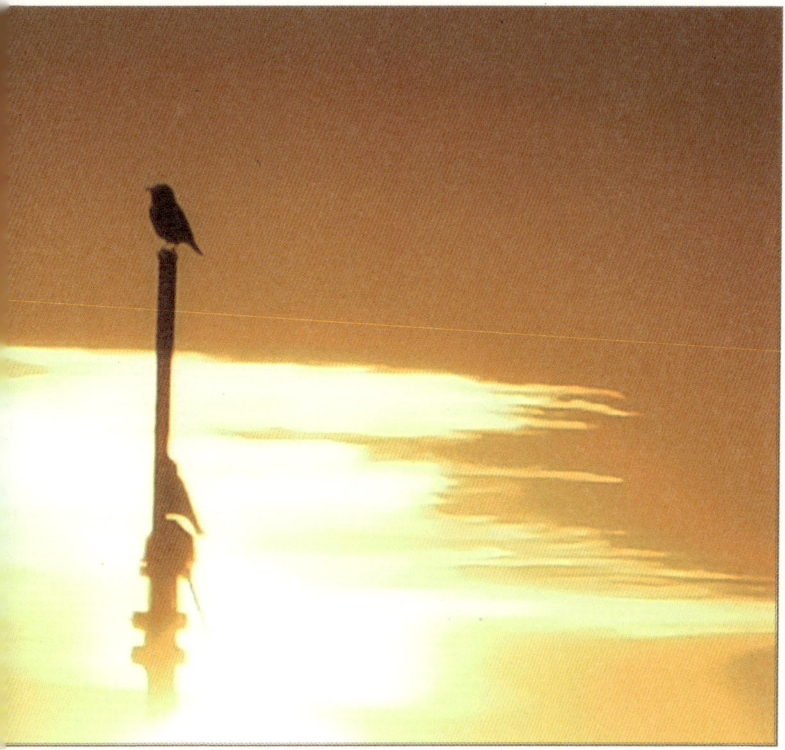

Part 2
悲：拔除眾生痛苦

無私的愛如寒冬暖陽,溫暖苦難人的身心。

——《靜思語·十在心路·伍》

Selfless love is like warm sunshine in the cold winter, bringing comfort to the bodies and minds of those in distress.

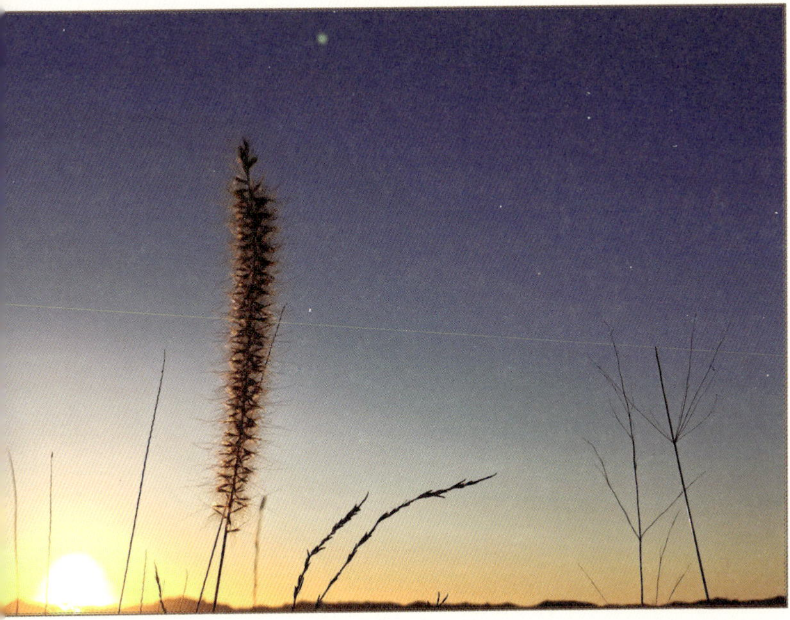

Part 2
悲：拔除眾生痛苦

發揮覺有情的愛,知己之福、知彼之苦。

——《靜思語·十在心路·柒》

Express love with mindfulness and compassion, understanding the blessings we have and the struggles of others.

Part 2
悲：拔除眾生痛苦

慈心期待天下人皆幸福，
悲心視天下苦難者爲親人，
無怨無悔、盡力救拔。

——《靜思語・十在心路・柒》

With loving-kindness, we wish for all people to find happiness. With compassion, we regard all those in suffering as family and do our best to help them, without complaint or regret.

Part 2
悲：拔除眾生痛苦

明是非、養慈悲，虔誠懺悔；人間菩薩愈密集，就能築出最穩固的人心堤防，防範災難。

——《靜思語・十在心路・柒》

Clearly distinguish right from wrong, nurture compassion, and practice sincere repentance. When more Living Bodhisattvas gather in the world, a steadfast dam of compassion can be built to protect against calamity.

Part 2
悲：拔除眾生痛苦

菩薩就在他、你、我之間——走入苦難人群、伸手救拔，就是人間菩薩。

——《靜思語‧十在心路‧柒》

Bodhisattvas reside among us—in them, in you, and in me. To go among the suffering and extend a hand in aid, is to be a Living Bodhisattva.

Part 2
悲：拔除眾生痛苦

「慈悲」的具體表現,就是走入人群,濟助貧老孤殘。

——《靜思語・十在心路・玖》

The tangible act of compassion is to go among people and assist the impoverished, the elderly, the orphaned, and the disabled.

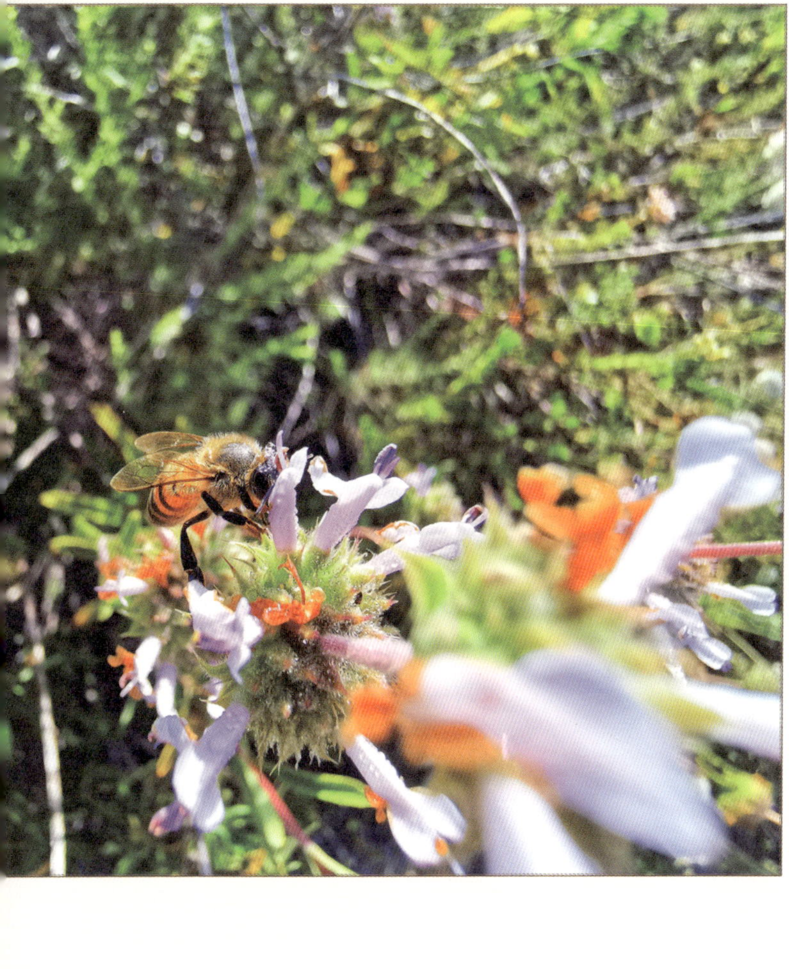

Part 2
悲：拔除眾生痛苦

布施有形物資,彌補困乏之苦;付出無形愛心,膚慰心靈苦難。

——《靜思語・十在心路・玖》

Giving material goods can lessen the suffering of scarcity; offering intangible love soothes the suffering of the mind.

Part 2
悲：拔除眾生痛苦

不辭勞苦的付出，便是「慈悲」。
　　　　　　　——《靜思小語1》

To willingly undergo hardship for the sake of helping others is compassion.

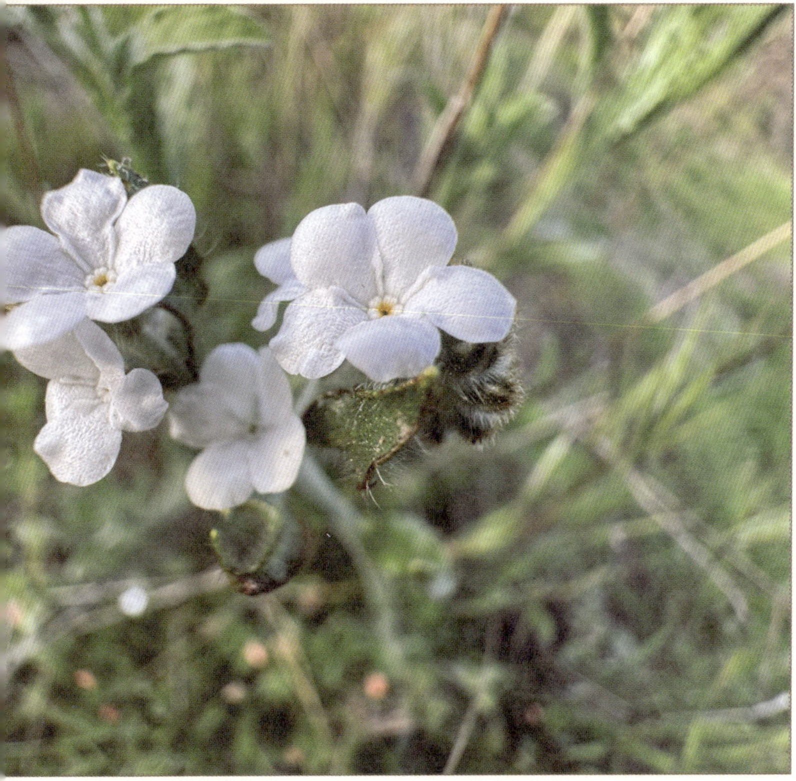

Part 2
悲：拔除眾生痛苦

用寧靜的心態,觀大地眾生相,
聽大地眾生聲。

—《靜思語・第一集》

We should observe and listen to all living creatures in the world with a calm and peaceful mind.

Part 2
悲:拔除眾生痛苦

解除人間的災難,一定要從改善人心做起。

——《靜思小語1》

To end the disasters of the world, we must transform and improve the human mind.

Part 2
悲：拔除眾生痛苦

在最需要的時刻，貼切的一分愛，就有很大的安撫力量。

——《靜思小語3》

In the hour of greatest need, empathic care brings great comfort.

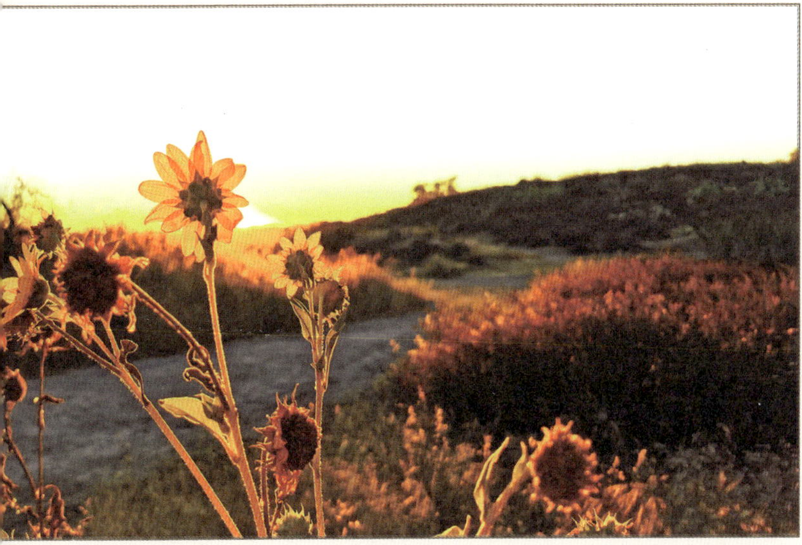

Part 2
悲：拔除眾生痛苦

感恩可以打開我們的心結,並且啟發我們的悲心。

——《靜思小語4》

Having gratitude can help us dissolve our inner afflictions and inspire our compassion.

219

Part 2
悲：拔除眾生痛苦

把氣憤的心境轉換為柔和，把柔和的心境再轉換為愛，如此，這個世界將日益完美。

——《靜思語·第一集》

Turn anger into gentleness, then turn gentleness into love. In this way, the whole world will become more perfect every day.

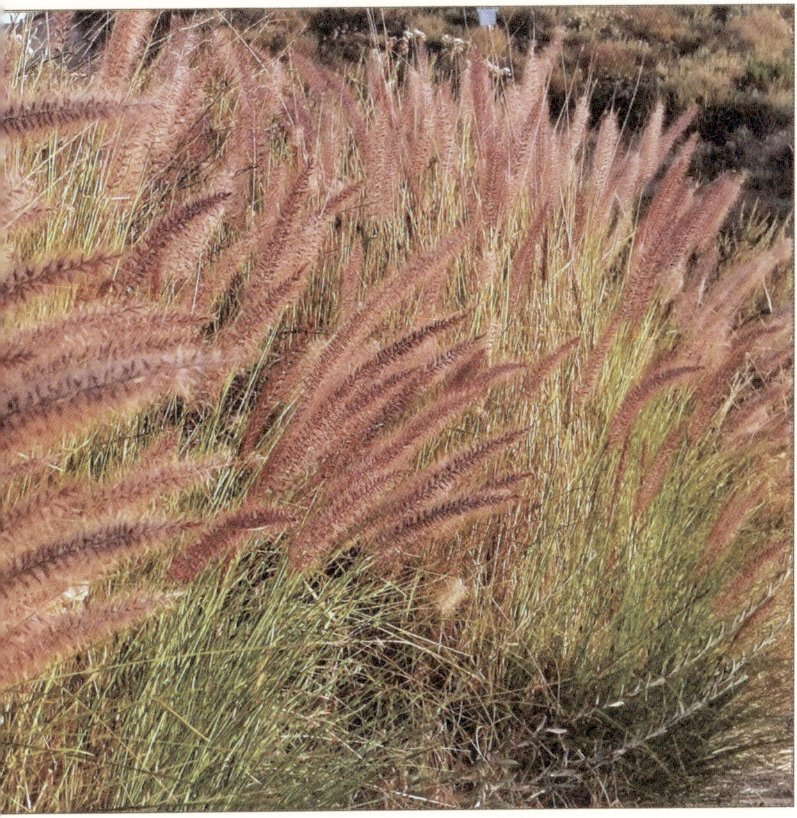

Part 2
悲:拔除眾生痛苦

眞正的解脫是在眾緣中付出而得，
也是在眾緣的煩惱中解脫。

——《靜思小語2》

True liberation is realized through unselfish giving for the benefit of mankind. It is also realized through the challenges of relationships with others.

Part 2
悲：拔除眾生痛苦

如果人人發揮慈悲心,即可形成「一眼觀時千眼觀,一手動時千手動」的「千手千眼觀世音菩薩」,並具足無量悲願的濟世力量。

——《靜思語・第二集》

If we all exercise our compassion, then we can work together like the thousand eyes and thousand hands of Guanyin Bodhisattva; when one eye see, one thousand eyes see, and when hand moves, one thousand hands move. Then we can tap into the boundless power of our compassionate vows and save the world.

後記

慈悲最本真的樣貌

蔡青兒

去年花蓮強震後，賓哥在美國第一時間傳來訊息關心：「台灣花蓮大地震，大家都好吧？上人及靜思精舍那邊沒事吧？」

我回：「賓哥好，感恩關心，花蓮靜思精舍都平安。精舍局部受損，人員均平安；目前在戶外安全地區辦公。上人正在戶外親自坐鎮指揮救災工作。昨天我跟上人報告靜思閱讀書軒的故事，還提到《善，最好的禮物》這本書裡面使用你的照片。上人問起你何時回來，並說他很喜歡你的照片，因為本身就很靜，而且意境很好，你拍的角度各方面都很不錯。我說你快回來了，有空的話再邀請你回精舍。」

賓哥回覆：「太好了！上人與大家都平安就好了。真的感恩你讓我受到了上人的祝福與關懷。這次回台若有緣分，當去花蓮再拜望上人。感恩與祝福大家平安吉祥。」

後　記

　　我說：「我覺得台灣有很多很多人造福、善念共振，上天庇護。要繼續造福、虔誠祈福。」

　　賓哥回我：「上人積福於人間，太偉大了！」

慈悲的內心世界映照出畫面之美

　　後來我跟賓哥說，如果他還有照片，都可以給我。因為之前兩本書《愛，最好的祝福》、《善，最好的禮物》，上人的靜思語搭配他的照片，大家都很喜歡。閱讀時可以從上人的靜思語感受到慈悲、慈祥與溫暖提醒，和自己的心靈做對話，還可以從照片中感受到賓哥慈悲的內心世界映照出的畫面之美。

　　賓哥跟我說，他這幾年拍的都是野花、野草，小到不行，立於天地之間，數量也很多。他想拍那些最弱小的生命，隨著季節的變化，發芽、茁壯、成長、繁衍，在風雨中依然綻放美麗與動人的樣貌。這些照片大都是手機拍的，附近整個

山區的春、夏、秋、冬都拍了,他很喜歡,捨不得刪除。

萬物都是有靈性的。賓哥的心意真美,關注到弱小的生命;受到賓哥關注的小花、小草,會綻放得很高興。

賓哥如此的慈悲有愛。這本書的書名《慈悲:時時歡喜,處處安身》,出自於上人的《靜思語·第二集》裡面的一句話:「時時保持快樂的心境,把快樂的氣氛散布給四周的人,此即『慈』;眾生有苦難能及時為其拔除,此即『悲』。」

我們在上人身上看到的,就是那份真正的慈悲;無緣大慈,同體大悲。

慈悲的法水,讓苦難之地能萌生新芽

二〇一三年十一月八日,世紀強颱海燕橫掃菲律賓,造成六千三百多人死亡、一千七百多人失蹤,三百四十多萬個家庭受到影響。首當其衝的重災區獨魯萬市,被形容為「棄

後 記

城」,放眼望去盡是斷垣殘壁。

當時上人正在台北關渡為一年一度的歲末祝福行腳,剛好有很多菲律賓慈濟志工幹部來台灣。我印象很深刻的是,小小的會客室裡,上人與菲律賓慈濟志工談起這個災難,並討論如何救災。上人講到災民時的那份不捨,彷彿他正親坐現場,親身感受到了災民的苦及煎熬。上人呼籲大家要趕緊投入行動,也呼籲全球慈濟人全動員,給予最重要的幫助。上人一邊講,好幾次語帶哽咽,在一旁的我也忍不住流下淚。我自己在菲律賓出生、長大,但聽到上人那份要救拔疾苦的悲憫之心時,全場沒有人不動容。

這份慈悲的力量,讓原本受傷的土地跟人們,得到最大的幫助。這個地方人人安居樂業,更有許多人成為慈濟志工,從手心向上變成手心向下,去照顧更多需要的人。在上人身上看到慈悲的力量。

這正是《法華經 · 藥草喻品》所說:「如彼大雲,雨於

一切卉木叢林及諸藥草,如其種性,具足蒙潤,各得生長。」慈悲的法水,平等潤澤,讓苦難之地也能萌生新芽。

靜思書軒有很多小志工,年齡從三歲到十二歲,在他們身上也看到慈悲的力量。他們用純真的話語詮釋慈悲:「吃菜菜還會再長,吃肉肉,牠就不會再蹦蹦跳跳了。」「如果吃雞,雞媽媽會找不到雞寶寶。」

這些童言童語,恰是慈悲最本真的樣貌——對生命的尊重與疼惜。

願我們都能以一念慈悲心,

照見世間苦難,化為行動的力量,

讓每一個生命,都能在愛與善的循環中,

找到安身立命之處。

人與土地 52

慈悲：時時歡喜，處處安身——靜思心靈小語

作　　者—釋證嚴
攝　　影—李屏賓
英文翻譯—Dharma as Water Team, Tzu Chi USA
特約主編—吳毓珍
副 主 編—陳萱宇
主　　編—謝翠鈺
行銷企劃—鄭家謙
封面設計—Javick 工作室
美術編輯—Javick 工作室

董 事 長—趙政岷
出 版 者—時報文化出版企業股份有限公司
　　　　　108019 台北市和平西路三段二四○號七樓
　　　　　發行專線—（○二）二三○六六八四二
　　　　　讀者服務專線—○八○○二三一七○五
　　　　　　　　　　　（○二）二三○四七一○三
　　　　　讀者服務傳真—（○二）二三○四六八五八
　　　　　郵　　撥—一九三四四七二四時報文化出版公司
　　　　　信　　箱—一○八九九 台北華江橋郵局第九九信箱

時報悅讀網— http://www.readingtimes.com.tw
法律顧問—理律法律事務所 陳長文律師、李念祖律師
印刷—勤達印刷有限公司
初版一刷—二○二五年四月十八日
初版二刷—二○二五年六月十日
定價—新台幣五五○元
缺頁或破損的書，請寄回更換

靜思人文
JING SI CULTURE
http://www.jingsi.org
http://www.tzuchi.org

慈悲：時時歡喜，處處安身：靜思心靈小語 / 釋證嚴著.
-- 初版. -- 臺北市：時報文化出版企業股份有限公司,
2025.04
　面；　公分. -- (人與土地；52)
中英對照
ISBN 978-626-419-337-5(精裝)

1.CST: 佛教說法 2.CST: 佛教教化法

225.4　　　　　　　　　　　　　　114002794

ISBN 978-626-419-337-5
Printed in Taiwan

時報文化出版公司成立於一九七五年，
並於一九九九年股票上櫃公開發行，於二○○八年脫離中時集團非屬旺中，
以「尊重智慧與創意的文化事業」為信念。